RE-THINKING GREGORY OF NYSSA

Re-thinking Gregory of Nyssa

Edited by
Sarah Coakley

Blackwell
Publishing

© 2003 by Blackwell Publishing Ltd

First published as volume 18, number 4 of *Modern Theology*, 2002

350 Main Street, Malden, MA 02148-5018, USA
108 Cowley Road, Oxford OX4 1JF, UK
550 Swanston Street, Carlton South, Melbourne, Victoria 3053, Australia
Kurfürstendamm 57, 10707 Berlin, Germany

First published 2003 by Blackwell Publishing Ltd

Reprinted 2004

Library of Congress Cataloging-in-Publication Data has been applied for

ISBN 1-40510-637-9

A catalogue record for this title is available from the British Library.

Set by Advance Typesetting Ltd
Printed and bound in the United Kingdom
by MPG books Ltd, Bodmin, Cornwall

For further information on
Blackwell Publishing, visit our website:
http://www.blackwellpublishing.com

CONTENTS

CONTENTS

1

INTRODUCTION—GENDER, TRINITARIAN ANALOGIES, AND THE PEDAGOGY OF *THE SONG*

SARAH COAKLEY

Introduction: Nyssa Studies in Transition

No one who works in systematic theology, let alone in patristic studies, can have failed to notice the recent upsurge of interest in the work and thought of Gregory of Nyssa (c. 330–c. 395), the youngest of the so-called "Cappadocian Fathers", and in many ways the most subtle and intriguing. The reasons for this renewed interest are arguably three-fold. First, it corresponds to the notable resurgence of trinitarianism in post-modern theology in general, and hence to a re-examination of the place of Nyssa in the supposed founding of a distinctively "Eastern" trinitarian tradition.[1] Second—and for the most part so far in disjunction from this first focus—there is the interest spawned by Nyssa's fascinating views on asceticism and desire (matters which now often fall under the rubric of "gender theory").[2] And finally—and again in somewhat problematic connection to the other two foci—there is a new appreciation of Nyssa's distinctive apophaticism, another theme re-invigorated by the interests of post-modernity.[3] By and large, however, these three interests have tended not to find integration in any one author: they are "fragments" that the post-modern theologian has gathered into her basket *ad libitum*, whether in search of the doctrinal renewal of "orthodoxy" (at one end of the spectrum), or of the destruction of repressive "gender binaries" (at the other).

It is in this rather confused context that this collection of essays on Gregory has been brought together to mark a new moment in the interpretation of his

Sarah Coakley
Harvard Divinity School, 14 Divinity Avenue, Cambridge, MA 02138, USA

oeuvre, one that the contributors believe holds creative promise both for the patristic exegete and for the systematician. But there is both death and life here: death, because a significant portion of our work is involved in the tolling of the final funeral bell on a *misreading* of Gregory's trinitarianism that has been peculiarly long-standing and pernicious for ecumenical understanding; and life, because the re-reading that we jointly propose suggests not only opportunities for renewed ecumenical understanding, but an integrated approach to Gregory's work in which the false disjunctions of modernity ("theology"/"spirituality", "doctrine"/"ascetical theology", "philosophy"/"exegesis", even "sex"/"gender") may be laid aside in aid of a deeper appreciation of his significance and creativity.

A brief, synthetic overview of the main themes of this collection—and their interconnection—is in order first (Section I). Here I shall merely provide a template into which the various essays may be slotted, although their distinctive emphases should not be lost sight of in the detailed reading. To undertake this task I shall need to allude to some features of the *Redaktionsgeschicte* which has led to the misreadings of Gregory we have inherited. From here (Section II) I shall turn to an explication of some proposed new exegetical principles of my own for the future study of Gregory's doctrinal *Nachlass* in general, and especially of his trinitarianism, and so indicate at the outset of this collection (Section III) how questions of eroticism and "gender" (a modern appellation, to be sure) fall squarely within the reach of what the trinitarian exegete of Gregory must attend to. Whilst not all the contributors need necessarily concur with my reading here, it is certain that the cumulative effect of the essays will stir new thoughts about the appropriate way of *teaching* Gregory's views on doctrinal matters. If his own pedagogy is a purified "pedagogy of desire", we may well enquire what are the implications for an equivalent contemporary exposition, what—that is—are the *ascetical* requirements for a mature appreciation of dogmatic questions. That is a question that this volume leaves for the reader's consideration.

I: The End of the "de Régnon" Paradigm, and What Lies Beyond

The first purpose of this collection of essays, however, is to call radically into question the adequacy of a long-established, and oft-repeated, account of the significance of Gregory of Nyssa's contribution to the trinitarian debates of the late-fourth century. That text-book account is familiar to those in the English-speaking (and especially Anglican) world from the pages of such indispensable introductory guides as Prestige, Kelly, Hardy and Richardson, and Wiles.[4] For all that these authors differ in emphasis and detail in their analyses, they share the presumption that Gregory's text *Ad Ablabium: On Why there are Not Three Gods* (written c. 375) is a crucial one—if not the crucial one—for understanding Gregory's specific advance on previous trinitarian thinking. They point to his supposed clarification of the meaning of *hypostasis*, and his drawing of the distinction (in terms of the analogy of individualizing *versus* generic characteristics applied to the visible world) between the three *hypostaseis* and the more encompassing divine *ousia*. No one would deny— least of all I—that this argument represents a significant technical advance in attempting to ward off Arianism and Sabellianism simultaneously, although the precise force, success, and significance of the argument has been debated,[5] and is given new adjudication by Ayres, Barnes and Turcescu in this volume. What is more puzzling, however (granted the amount of writing that Gregory devoted to the matter of the Trinity in his lifetime), is the stranglehold that the *Ad Ablabium*, with its opening analogy of three men proffered initially by Ablabius, has come to hold in this textbook account. Granted that the *Letter 38* (previously ascribed to Basil, and covering much of the same philosophical ground) also utilizes the analogy, this too has been marked out for (suitably excerpted) anthologizing (as in Wiles and Santer).[6] The dominance of the three men analogy, one may note, is a matter not without interest to those concerned with questions of *gender* in theological utterance, although perhaps unsurprisingly it occurs to none of the textbook writers I have mentioned to comment on that implication. (Gregory of course uses *anthropoi* rather than *andres* in the three men analogy, but his examples of proper names are all male ones.) I shall return to the matter of gender and the Trinity in the last section of this introductory essay.

On closer inspection of the text of the *Ad Ablabium*, however, it turns out that this supposedly crucial analogy of three men is one that Gregory himself sees as limited in its significance, and indeed distinctly misleading if construed without the necessarily *apophatic* effacement required of any analogical move from the human to the divine realms. "We", writes Gregory, "following the suggestions of Holy Scripture, have learned that [God's] nature cannot be named and is ineffable". Thus, although we can distinguish between "right" and "wrong" conceptions of the deity, we cannot "*explain*" the divine nature.[7] "Our feeble powers of reason", Gregory has already said, are almost certainly not adequate to the problem in hand; we may have to fall back on the authority of "tradition".[8] Immediately, then, the question of the status of Gregory's negative theology impinges on the assessment of his trinitarianism. A further consideration is that Gregory offers many other, mutually corrective, analogies for the Trinity alongside the three men one, both in the two texts already mentioned, and elsewhere, even in his apologetic and catechetical writings: there is a spring as source of water (repeatedly in the anti-Eunomian writings and again in the *Ad Ablabium*); the grape and the wine, again in the anti-Eunomian corpus; gold and coins in the *Ad Ablabium*; the rainbow and the chain in *Ep*. 38; and an interesting psychological analogy of breath and mind in ch. 2 of the *Catechetical Oration* which we might more readily expect from Augustine.[9] Even this list does not exhaust Gregory's repertoire, as Hart's essay in this volume—drawing on a number of un-translated writings—amply testifies. So this diversity in itself should already cause us to question a simplistic account of Gregory's trinitarian achievement based only on one visual model, and only one (supposedly key) text.

But *why*, then, the continuing, regnant emphasis on the "three men" in the literature I have cited? Could it be, as an important earlier article by Michel René Barnes[10] has documented fully (and André de Halleux had already earlier suggested[11]) that the lurking influence of de Régnon's classic work on the Trinity[12] has fixated both Easterners and Westerners, and for over a century now, on a reading of Gregory as "starting from the three and proceeding to the one"; and so—according to a further elaboration, most famously associated with John Zizioulas[13]—normatively instantiating the so-called "social Trinity of the East", a "communitarian" understanding in which "personhood" is somehow *prior* to "substance"? This is a view that has certainly both fuelled and bedevilled ecumenical exchange in recent decades; and it is ironic to find Lossky at points directly dependent on de Régnon on this issue, and Zizioulas on Prestige![14] To have the "West" attacked by the "East" on a reading of the Cappadocians that was ultimately spawned by a French Jesuit is a strange irony. But this reading has both drawn on, and further cemented, the dominance (visually and imaginatively speaking) of the personalistic "three men" analogy for this purportedly "Eastern" view. It is precisely this reading, and this dominance, that Ayres's and Barnes' essays, taken together, crucially question here. Whilst Ayres gives a detailed new reading of the *Ad Ablabium* which attempts finally to lay to rest the "de Régnon" reading, Barnes provides a detailed account of the developing relationship between Gregory's vision of the individual "self" and of trinitarian "persons" (*hypostaseis*), arguing strongly against the smuggling of modern "personalism" into the reading of the latter. The trinitarian persons are neither prototypes of Enlightenment "individualism", *nor* exemplars of a "personalism" that somehow precedes and transcends "substance" (a false disjunction). Rather, the most important point of contact between Gregory's human psychology and his trinitarianism (even allowing for apophatic difference) lies in the notion of the unity of *will*: in the Trinity of divine "persons" *one* will pervades the ordered flow of divine activity, just as in Gregory's doctrine of the human, "psychology takes its fundamental shape from a concern for the integrity of the will in its action".

The effects of this re-reading, and its extension of consideration to a much wider collection of Nyssa's texts (even within the apologetic/catechetical *genre*) than the "de Régnon paradigm" tended to encourage, is to open up possibilities of East/West *rapprochement* that have seemingly long been despaired of. It was thus a conscious editorial policy to invite into this exchange the perspectives of Orthodox (Turcescu, Hart), Roman Catholic (Barnes, Laird, Daley) and Anglican (Ayres, Coakley) scholars, who—remarkably, one might think—have converged on a re-assessment of Gregory's significance as one refusing to be "boxed" into the stereotype of an "Easterner" rudely confronting the supposed trinitarian "mentalism" of "the West". Whilst Congar, in his great trilogy *I Believe in the Holy Spirit*,[15] had already drawn attention to the misleading nature of this disjunctive myth, it has taken a long time effectively to dislodge it. Especially important in this collection, then, are the contributions of the two Orthodox scholars: Turcescu challenging Zizioulas's polemical reading of the Cappadocians as supposedly routing "Western" essentialism, and Hart drawing attention to the profound commonalities between Gregory's and Augustine's trinitarian instincts. We can only hope that this collection will lead to further mutual enrichment and understanding, both East and West, of the formative patristic periods of trinitarian thinking.

So far I have focused on the primary constellating theme of this volume, its careful re-reading of Gregory's trinitarianism through the axis of (1) an extended range of apologetic and catechetical texts (beyond the *Ad Ablabium* and *Ep. 38*); (2) diverse controlling "analogies" (beyond the "three men"); and (3) chastened "modernistic" assumptions about *either* Cartesian "individualism" *or* relational "personhood". The crucial significance (4) of taking Gregory's apophatic sensibilities into account in this re-reading has also been noted, as has the possible implications for East/West ecumencial re-engagement (5). But this is not quite all that this collection undertakes in its suggestions about "re-thinking" Gregory of Nyssa. For to this list of distinctive themes we now should add: (6) the importance of bringing Gregory's (unduly neglected) christology into relation with his trinitarianism, especially in connection with the supposed "clarification" he brought to bear—trinitarianly—on the meaning of "person"; (7) the significance of Gregory's wider *exegetical* corpus for the assessment and understanding of his doctrinal contribution; concomitantly, (8) the importance of Gregory's *ascetical* programme as a matrix for the understanding of his doctrinal contribution; and finally, and also relatedly, (9) the intrinsic significance of Gregory's views about the transformation of human "desire" (a matter that contemporaneously shelters under the—perhaps misleading—rubrics of "eroticism" and "gender") in his perception of our capacity for transformation into the trinitarian God. Here we glimpse the possibility of the integration of the varying points of interest recently aroused in Nyssa scholarship that I mentioned at the outset.

On point (6) in this list, Brian Daley's programmatic article in this collection is especially important, raising as it does the issue of the undue neglect of Gregory's christology on account of its failure to conform to what may be called the "false-starts or approximations" model of Grillmeier's reading of pre-Chalcedonian christology. Gregory's christology is indeed peculiarly hard to classify from the perspective of the fifth-century Antiochene/Alexandrian dialectic; ingeniously, he seems to incorporate aspects of both extremes. Yet much work remains to be done on the relation of his unusual reading of *kenotic* christology as it coheres with his subtle trinitarian perception of the nature of "person".[16] This collection can only raise the possibility of that future work, and of a more detailed assessment of the coherence of Gregory's christological contribution.

As for the remaining three themes ((7)–(9), above), while other contributors allude to them, it is largely Laird and I who are concerned to explore them, and—in my case—especially to underscore their intrinsic connection to the other themes of the volume. Laird's essay looks at the language of "desire" in Gregory (admittedly confusing in its lack of semantic consistency), charts its relation to his apophaticism, and explores his programme for the ascetical transformation of passion, especially as illuminated by his late work, the commentary on *The Song*. My own addition to this, in what remains of this introductory essay, is to attempt to show the significance of that material for our understanding of the full impact of Gregory's trinitarian vision. If I am right, then no one should be teaching or expounding Gregory's views on the Trinity without also explaining his theory of "desire" for God, and his unique charting of the shifts in (what we would now call) "gender" perception—both in oneself and in God—that seemingly inexorably attend the ascetical trans-formation of that desire. If this is granted, then here is a rich dimension to Gregory's trinitarian thinking which, as far as I know, is completely ignored in expository textbook accounts, but which, once we are released from the false dominance of the "three men" model, may rightly find its due.

But this is to jump ahead to the material from the commentary on *The Song* to be explored in my final section. In preparation for that exposition, I need to prepare the ground (especially in relation to points (7) and (8), above), by enunciating some general principles for an integrated reading of Nyssa that might transcend some of the classic hermeneutical disjunctions of "modernity".

II: *Exegesis and Doctrine in Gregory's Corpus*

Before turning to the salient trinitarian passages in the commentary, then, let me mention some overarching principles that, as I see it, should rightly guide our use of Gregory's *exegetical* writings in the explication of his full doctrinal position on the Trinity. Here are seven such principles for reflec-tion, which cut across all of the distinctive themes in this volume that I have just outlined.

(i) First, surely only a false disjunction between exegesis and philosophical thinking, or between (so-called) "spirituality" and "theology", would prevent us from utilizing the commentaries as a source of insight for Gregory's doctrinal position *in toto*. In ignoring the exegetical material the textbooks already provide but a partial understanding of Gregory's full trinitarian contribution. In this light, it is odd to say, as Daniélou does of Gregory's late exegetical writings: "Once freed from administrative burdens and the heat of *theological* controversy, Gregory now turned himself wholly towards the life of the *spirit*."[17] As Ronald Heine too has noted in his dissertation on the *Life of Moses*, this is a questionable diremption.[18] These late writings contain no less "theological" content than their predecessors, despite their (often very great) differences of *genre* and intended audience.

(ii) Secondly, we must however take account of the complexification that the exposition of doctrine does not unfold for Gregory on a *flat plane*, so to speak. He is regularly wont to remind us that different audiences, and different occasions, will require different sorts of skill on the part of the theologian. In the famous opening passage of the *Catechetical Oration*, for instance, Gregory underscores that one would rightly shift one's Christian pedagogical tactics depending on whether one's interlocutors were Jews, "Hellenists", Manicheans, or certain sorts of Christian "heretic".[19] He also regularly uses the metaphor of the doctor's varying prescriptions to indicate the diversity of "cures" needed in doctrinal disputes.[20] By implication, we should expect the same principle of diversification of purpose to attach to the explication of trinitarian doctrine —as indeed the opening sections of the *Catechetical Oration* on the Trinity go on to testify.

(iii) However, by implication also, Gregory's understanding of "spiritual ascent" (as adumbrated rather differently in the *Inscriptions on the Psalms, The Life of Moses,* and *The Song*) suggests a doctrinal progression and deepening in the life of each individual Christian over time. Stages of spiritual growth are thus no less levels of doctrinal apprehension; we should not expect the careful apologetic rejoinder to a possible charge of tritheism (as in the *Ad Ablabium*) to be the last word in the trinitarian "case", but rather the movement "from Dove to Dove" which marks the mature apprehension of incorporation into the divine life itself.[21] Exegesis of *The Song* constitutes the apex of spiritual and doctrinal apprehension, as Gregory, following Origen (following the rabbis), expounds at length in the first *Homily*.[22]

(iv) Certain sorts of polemical context demand philosophical precision; but ultimately philosophy is *subordinate* to Scripture. (Gregory makes this point, for instance, in vivid terms in *The Life of Moses*, likening the "daughter of Pharaoh" to vain philosophy—always in labour but never giving birth.[23]) Thus we should, by the same token, expect to find *deeper* insight, ultimately, into trinitarian doctrine in the exegetical writings than in the polemical or philosophical—even though we must beware here of re-forcing a disjunction that we are attempting to overcome: Gregory's exegetical writings can and do contain polemical modes, and *vice versa*. Nonetheless, I am suggesting here that we consider coming to Gregory's polemical tracts on the Trinity with our eyes already on *The Song*. To read Gregory as a somewhat failed Oxford Greats man, someone whose philosophical acumen deserted him under stress (as seems, one sometimes feels, to be Christopher Stead's mode of critique in relation to the *Ad Ablabium*[24]), is to miss this major complexification. For as Gregory underscores (also in Origen's train), Scripture does not easily or quickly deliver her "mystical" insights. A philosophical manoeuvre may be readily accessible to the pagan interlocutor; an exegetical manoeuvre less obviously so. The insights of "faith" (*pistis*) in the technical, epistemological sense that Gregory uses for this term,[25] are not ones arrived at without inner transformation precisely in relation to Scriptural norms.

(v) The central hold of apophaticism in Gregory's trinitarian exposition in polemical contexts has already been underscored. A careful reading of the *Ad Ablabium*, as we have already intimated (and Ayres demonstrates in detail), must take this line of Gregory's argument more seriously than many modern commentators have. From here we need to relate that line of thinking to its deeper, and more "affective", enunciation in the exegetical writings. In *The Song*, that feature of noetic darkness as regards God's "essence" is all the more marked: here it is only the "hand of the bridegroom" that reaches out from the darkness to draw us to him: "'My beloved has put his hand through the door'", writes Gregory, "[for] Human nature is not able to contain the infinite unbounded divine nature" (*Cant.* 11).[26]

(vi) The effect of the established hold of the apophatic dimension at the level of *The Song* seems to be a certain loosening up of imagery where trinitarian "analogies" are concerned—a willingness to rehearse a veritable chaos of different visual symbolisms for the *hypostaseis*, which, if falsely pressed, would certainly result in absurdities (and we shall come to some examples of this from *The Song* shortly). The difference here from the carefully chosen (but mutually corrective) analogies of the more polemical and catechetical writings is instructive, and—I presume—advised.

(vii) Matters of "sex" and "gender" (in modern appellation)[27] are to the fore in *The Song* where questions of incorporation into the life of the Trinity are at stake. This is of course to be expected granted the pervasive dominance of the erotic metaphor in *The Song*. Even so, as Verna Harrison's work has so illuminatingly exposed,[28] Gregory takes more surprising risks in this area than we might expect.

If we may grant the acceptance, or at least entertainment, of these exegetical principles, let us now look at how these risks specifically relate to *trinitarian* exposition in *The Song*.

III: Trinitarian Images in the Commentary on The Song

When we read Gregory's commentary with trinitarian questions in mind, the first thing that one notes is his happy disregard for what we may call "orthodox" precision. It is a striking feature of this work that individual divine "persons" can be spoken of as "acting in quite different roles",[29] with the Father's origination of those roles being merely left implicit. Thus, for instance, Gregory will speak of Christ as the "nuptial torch of the Holy Spirit's splendor" (*Cant.* 13);[30] or about how we may smell the "scent of the divine perfumes" by "drawing in the good odor of Christ by an inhalation of the Spirit" (*Cant.* 1).[31] Despite this freedom, even apparent carelessness, the implicit underlying pattern remains that which was set out in the *Ad Ablabium* about the ordered causality of the divine operations *ad extra*—originating in the Father, and extending via the Son to the Spirit.

When we look for more lengthy or developed expositions of the Trinity's operations in Gregory's *Song*, four are to be found in the Commentary, each characterized by unusually visual and imaginative complexity, and each concerned with the pressure towards incorporative union with the divine. Of these, two I shall mention only briefly here (for reasons of conciseness): in *Homily* 12, the Spirit is the wind sent by the Father in the sails of the vessel (the Church) that moves to contemplate the Word, and in which the "Song's text" acts as "pilot"[32]—an elaborated nautical image which it is interesting to compare with the *internalized* "wind" and "word" of the psychological analogy at the beginning of the *Catechetical Oration*. In *Homily* 15, in contrast, in the course of a reflection on the Johannine farewell discourse on the union of Father and Son (John 17:21), the Spirit, interestingly, becomes the bond (*sundetikon*) of union between Father and Son, characterized as "glory" (*doxa*) and overflowing to the Church: "[Christ] received this glory which he already had before the world's beginning when he clothed himself with human nature. Because his human nature was glorified by the Spirit, such a relationship in the glory of the Spirit is distributed to everyone united with Christ, beginning with the disciples."[33] With this idea of the Holy Spirit as bond between Father and Son and as then overflowing to the church, we could hardly hope, perhaps, for a more "Western", Augustinian, trinitarian reflection—something that presents yet another challenge to the textbook stereotypes of so-called "Eastern" and "Western" Trinities.

But it is the two remaining (developed) trinitarian passages in *The Song* that I wish to focus upon in closing, for they both relate fascinatingly to questions of "gender" and the Trinity, and thus take us back to the undermining of the purported hegemony of the "three men" analogy. Both these passages are to be found in *Homily* 4. The first is a direct, but interestingly gender-modified, reflection on the incorporative theme of Romans 8, where Gregory is speaking of the bride's transformation into a "lily":

> Having thus become a flower, the soul is not injured by thorny temptations in her transformation into lily; she forgets the people and the house of her [sc. false] father and looks to her true Father. Therefore, she is named *sister* of the Son, having been introduced by the Spirit of adoption into this relationship and released from fellowship with the daughters of the false father. And so she becomes still more sublime and gazes at the mystery through dove's eyes. I mean she does this by the Spirit of prophecy.[34]

Because Gregory is here charting the highest (and third) stage in the ascent to God, it is crucial for him that the soul/bride is figured as "feminine", as receptive to the bridegroom's advances. The necessary gender fluidities and reversals of this ascent are already vividly spelled out in *Homily* 1, as Verna

Harrison's work has so well elucidated.[35] What is striking in this *Homily*, then, is the exegetical freedom with which Gregory superimposes the *female* "sister" on the Pauline narrative of adoptive sonship through the Spirit.

In the same *Homily* 4, we find our last, and most alluring and complex trinitarian allegory (a purple passage also commented on by Laird, *intra*, and finding an interesting short counterpart in Gregory's commentary on Psalm 3 in his *Commentary on the Inscriptions on the Psalms*[36]). Here the ("feminine") soul/bride is wounded by the arrow of divine love and then in turn becomes another arrow ready to be shot by the divine bowman.[37] Superimposed on this (already shifting) imagery is the *Song*'s theme (*Song* 2. 5–6) of the lover's left hand under the head of the bride and his right hand receiving her body. When we untangle these different, even chaotically-related, images, we have the Father as the archer, the Son as the arrow, and the Spirit as that in which the arrow is dipped. The arrow penetrates the soul with the wound of love, just as the Son as the bridegroom also penetrates, takes possession, of the bride. But the bride then herself *becomes* an extension or replication of the Son's arrow, since she has been allowed to "participate" in his "eternal incorruptibility".[38]

Of this remarkable passage, von Balthasar comments, in *Presence and Thought*: "The mystical level achieved by the soul [here] has definitely gone *beyond* the 'philosophy of desire'."[39] Yet oddly von Balthasar does not spell out the implications for Gregory's *trinitarian* contribution. Let us however now draw those implications together in closing.

We started this introductory essay with some comments on the way in which a particular reading of the "three men" analogy of the *Ad Ablabium* had achieved a false dominance, both in certain English patristic textbooks, and in important ecumencial debates. Much of this volume is devoted to overturning, and replacing, that paradigm with a richer and fuller picture of Gregory's doctrine of God. I, in my turn, have been concerned to widen the scope of our understanding of the final *telos* of Gregory's more precise and philosophical trinitarian reflections. If I am right, they find their completion in his exegetical account of *The Song*, and supremely in the rich if chaotic images of incorporation into the life of the divine *energeia*. In this account, it is the *human* soul that must, by progression, undergo various gender shifts and transformations *en route* to this incorporation. Gender, being strictly not applicable to God, leaves God unaffected by these human transformations; but equally, we are freed up, at the level of *The Song*, to speak of God as "mother" provided literal-mindedness is strictly ruled out of court. As Gregory puts it in a famous passage in the seventh *Homily*, "Both terms [i.e., mother and father] mean the same, because the divine is neither male nor female".[40] If we return to the "three men" analogy with these deeper thoughts in mind, it will be abundantly clear, on grounds other than the strictly philosophical ones that Gregory is rehearsing in the *Ad Ablabium*, that we need a broader base from which to assess the full significance of Gregory's trinitarianism, and its fascinating—and we might say, necessary—connections to gender issues, than that provided by the often-misconstrued text of the *Ad Ablabium* alone. What, I have suggested, if a new pedagogy of Gregory's trinitarianism should *start* with the rich insights into incorporation into the life of the Trinity brought about by mature "faith" (*pistis*)? How then would we turn back to read the import of the earlier, more obviously polemical, discussions? The emphases and expectations, I suggest, would be significantly different from those of the old textbook account with which we started. Whilst we cannot deny the myriad differences of style and *genre* with which Gregory plays in his various works, and his often infuriatingly inconsistent modes of argument, it is the challenge laid down by these collected essays to consider a "re-thinking" of the relation of those works in the ways here described, and thereby to attempt an integration of what modernity has balefully dubbed Gregory's "spirituality", on the one hand, with his "theology" and "philosophy", on the other.

NOTES

1 See Gerald O'Collins, S.J., "The Holy Trinity: The State of the Questions", in S. T. Davis, D. Kendall, S.J., and G. O'Collins, S.J., eds, *The Trinity* (Oxford: Oxford University Press, 1999), pp. 1–25, for a survey of the recent upsurge of interest in trinitarian theology.

2 See Martin Laird's essay, *intra*, especially nn. 1–5, for relevant literature. Also see my "The Eschatological Body: Gender, Transformation and God", in *Powers and Submissions: Spirituality, Power and Gender* (Oxford: Blackwell Publishers, 2002), pp. 153–167.

3 See especially David Bentley Hart, "Beauty, Violence, and Infinity: A Question Concerning Christian Rhetoric", Ph.D. dissertation, University of Virginia, 1997, for an excellent new discussion of the differing assessments of Gregory's apophaticism in the work of Daniélou and Mühlenberg.

4 See G. L. Prestige, *God in Patristic Thought* (London: SPCK, 1952); J. N. D. Kelly, *Early Christian Doctrines* (London: A & C Black, orig. 1958; 5th. ed. 1977); E. R. Hardy (ed), with C. C. Richardson, *Christology of the Later Fathers* (London: SCM Press, 1954); M. F. Wiles, *The Making of Christian Doctrine* (Cambridge: Cambridge University Press, 1975).

5 On the question of the supposed "clarification" of the meaning of "hypostasis" by Gregory, see the important article by Joseph T. Lienhard, S.J., "*Ousia* and *Hypostasis*: The Cappadocian Settlement and the Theology of 'One *Hypostasis*'", in Davis, Kendall and O'Collins, eds (see n. 1), pp. 99–121, for an effective critique of that view. For an anticipation of some of the central themes of this collection, see also my "'Persons' in the 'Social' Doctrine of the Trinity: A Critique of Current Analytic Discussion", in ibid., pp. 123–144.

6 See the selection from *Ep.* 38 in M. F. Wiles and M. Santer (eds), *Documents in Early Christian Thought* (Cambridge: Cambridge University Press, 1975), pp. 31–35.

7 As translated in Hardy and Richardson (eds), p. 259.

8 Ibid., p. 257.

9 These differing analogies and their precise contexts are discussed in some detail in my article "'Persons' in the 'Social' Doctrine of the Trinity" (see n. 5). Also see the essays by Ayres and Barnes, *intra*, for close discussion of these varying analogies.

10 M. R. Barnes, "De Régnon Reconsidered", *Augustinian Studies* 26 (1995), pp. 51–79.

11 See A. de Halleux, *Patrologie et Oecuménisme: Recueil D'Études* (Leuven: Leuven University Press, 1990), chs. 5, 6.

12 T. de Régnon, S.J., *Études de théologie positive sur la sainté Trinité*, vol. 1 (Paris: Victor Retaux et fils, 1892); one must be cautious, however, of attributing all the "blame" of this cumulative misreading to de Régnon himself: for a careful assessment, see again M. R. Barnes' article (n. 10).

13 J. D. Zizioulas, *Being as Communion: Studies in Personhood and the Church* (Crestwood, NY: St. Vladimir's Seminary Press, 1985).
14 For Lossky's use of de Régnon, see again M. R. Barnes's article (n. 10); for Zizioulas's occasional appeals to Prestige, see *Being as Communion* (n. 13), 38n., 41n., 85n.
15 See Y. Congar, *I Believe in the Holy Spirit* (New York, NY: Crossroad Publishing Company, 1997), vol. III, pp. xvi–xviii. I am grateful to my Harvard pupil Philip McCosker for drawing my attention to this passage.
16 I have attempted a first assessment of Nyssa's unusual reading of Phil. 2 in a forthcoming paper, "Does *Kenosis* Rest on A Mistake?: Three *Kenotic* Models in Patristic Exegesis", given at Calvin College, June, 2002.
17 In the "Introduction" to H. Musurillo, S.J., *From Glory to Glory: Texts from Gregory of Nyssa's Mystical Writings* (Crestwood, NY: St. Vladimir's Seminary Press, 1995), p. 9, my emphasis.
18 See R. Heine, *Perfection in the Virtuous Life: A Study in the Relationship between Edification and Polemical Theology in Gregory of Nyssa's* De Vita Moysis (Cambridge, MA: Philadelphia Patristic Foundation, 1975).
19 See Hardy and Richardson (eds), pp. 268–286.
20 See, e.g., the repeated return to the metaphors of doctor, medicine and cure in Gregory's *Homilies on the Beatitudes*, trans. H. C. Graef, ACW (London: 1954), pp. 88–89, 91–92, 104, 117, 172.
21 See the section on this theme (illustrated from *The Song*) in H. Musurillo (n. 17), pp. 189–191.
22 See *Saint Gregory of Nyssa Commentary on the Song of Songs*, trans. Casimir McCambley OCSO (Brookline, MA: Hellenic College Press, 1987), pp. 43–56.
23 *The Life of Moses*, trans. A. J. Malherbe and E. Ferguson (New York: Paulist Press, 1978), p. 57. For a sustained recent discussion of Gregory's evolving views on philosophy and the intellect, see Alden A. Mosshammer, "Gregory of Nyssa and Christian Hellenism", *Studia Patristica* 32 (1997), pp. 170–195.
24 See, for instance, G. C. Stead, "Ontologie und Terminologie bei Gregor von Nyssa", in eds H. Dörrie, M. Altenburger, U. Schramm, *Gregor von Nyssa und die Philosophie* (Leiden: E. J. Brill, 1976), pp. 107–127; also idem, "Why Not Three Gods?", in H. R. Drobner and C. Klock, eds, *Studien zu Gregor von Nyssa und der ChristlichenI Spätantike* (Leiden: E. J. Brill, 1990), pp. 149–163.
25 For a sustained treatment of this theme of *pistis* in Gregory, see Martin Laird, "The Grasp of Faith: Union and Knowledge in Gregory of Nyssa", Ph.D. thesis, University of London, 1999.
26 *Commentary* (n. 22), p. 208.
27 This distinction has itself become contentious in post-modern feminist theory, and is not of course utilized by Gregory himself. It is an intriguing question whether Gregory provides some of the necessary resources for overcoming this ("modern") disjunction, in a way that ironically anticipates some of the features of Judith Butler's current feminist theorizing. On this comparison, see my "The Eschatological Body" (n. 2, above).
28 See V. E. F. Harrison, "Male and Female in Cappadocian Theology", *Journal of Theological Studies* 41 (1990), pp. 441–471; and eadem, "Gender, Generation and Virginity in Cappadocian Theology", *Journal of Theological Studies* 47 (1996), pp. 38–68.
29 This phrase is from an unpublished paper by my Harvard pupil, Francis C.-W. Yip, "The Trinity and Christian Life in the Dogmatic and Spiritual Writings of Gregory of Nyssa". I am indebted to Yip for first having trawled the text of *The Song* for trinitarian passages at my suggestion. I acknowledge my gratitude to him for identifying the key passages which I also mention here.
30 *Commentary* (n. 22), p. 236.
31 Ibid., p. 52.
32 Ibid., p. 213.
33 Ibid., pp. 275–276.
34 Ibid., pp. 97–98.
35 See "Gender, Generation and Virginity" (n. 28).
36 Gregory of Nyssa, *Commentary on the Inscriptions of the Psalms*, trans. Casimir McCambley OCSO (Brookline, MA: Hellenic College Press, 1994), pp. 102–103.
37 *Commentary on the Song of Songs* (n. 22), pp. 103–104.

38   Ibid., p. 103.
39   H. U. von Balthasar, *Presence and Thought: Essay on the Religious Philosophy of Gregory of Nyssa* (San Francisco, CA: Ignatius Press, 1995), p. 160, my emphasis.
40   *Commentary* (n. 22), p. 145.

This paper was first presented, in an earlier version, at the Oxford Patristics Conference, August 1999; I am grateful to those who commented on it on that occasion. I would also like to express my thanks to all the contributors to this volume, and especially to my Harvard colleague Nicholas Constas, for much assistance and stimulating exchange in the preparation of these essays. My thanks too to two Harvard students, Todd Billings and Philip McCosker, for their speedy and efficient collection of bibliographical materials.

2

ON NOT THREE PEOPLE: THE FUNDAMENTAL THEMES OF GREGORY OF NYSSA'S TRINITARIAN THEOLOGY AS SEEN IN *TO ABLABIUS: ON NOT THREE GODS*

LEWIS AYRES

> [T]he sacred company of the prophets and Patriarchs ... from the names which express the manifold variety of his power, lead men, as by the hand, to the understanding of the divine nature, making known to them the bare grandeur of the thought of God; while the question of His essence, as one which it is impossible to grasp ... they dismiss without any attempt at its solution.[1]

I: Introduction

There are two questions vital for those seeking to understand or appropriate the legacy of pro-Nicene theology: which themes in Gregory of Nyssa's Trinitarian theology do we assert to be fundamental?; which texts do we take to provide paradigmatic instances of that theology? The purpose of this essay is to argue for an answer to these questions, based on a close reading of his short text *To Ablabius: On Not Three Gods*.[2] I will argue that we should not attempt to understand Gregory by reference primarily to the development of particular terminological formulations (such as one *ousia*, three *hypostases*). Nor should we attempt to understand Gregory by reading his thought against the background of a division of pro-Nicene theologians into

Lewis Ayres
Candler School of Theology, Emory University, Atlanta, GA 30322, USA

general "eastern" and "western" groups according to their supposed preference for "beginning from" unity or diversity in the Godhead.[3] I will suggest
that Gregory's Trinitarian theology is best approached by focusing on the
ways in which he makes a particular contribution to the emergence of a pro-
Nicene "grammar" of divinity through developing his complex account of
divine power.

On the one hand, Gregory uses an account of God's unitary power,
activity and causality as the basis for approaching the paradox of the divine
diversity and unity; it is here that we find Gregory's fundamental understanding of the grammar of divinity. On the other hand, and also through
his deployment of power terminology, Gregory also offers an ontological
and epistemological foundation for human knowledge of God that he thinks
fundamental to pro-Nicene theology and which sets the stage for any
analogical description of the Godhead. These themes are the real core of
Gregory's Trinitarian theology. In this light Gregory's statements about the
irreducibility and yet unity of the divine persons can only be approached
through first exploring his account of the nature of human speech about God
and the cosmology that grounds that account. Only when we see how this
account of divine creative power and ontological difference grounds a vision
of human speech about God will we begin to see what it means for Gregory
to confess the incomprehensible unity of the incomprehensible and yet
irreducible distinct divine persons.

It may seem strange that I have chosen to focus on *On Not Three Gods*,
given that this text is often taken in modern writing as a paradigm of
Gregory's supposed commitment to "beginning" with divine plurality rather
than unity, or even as a paradigm of his supposed commitment to "social"
Trinitarian analogies.[4] However, I will argue that Gregory's purpose in this
text is actually to point the reader away from speculating about the "social"
analogy and towards the very themes I outlined in the previous paragraph
as the necessary context for exploring the divinity unity and diversity. Only
in this context can any analogy serve a useful function and be properly
deployed. Thus, I will argue, *On Not Three Gods* is paradigmatic only because
it offers a summary of the positions advocated in Gregory's extensive polemics
against Eunomius and in the *Catechetical Oration*—and indeed I would want
to argue that when a short summary of Gregory's account of the divine
nature is needed the latter text is probably the most useful. It is also noteworthy that despite the frequency with which *On Not Three Gods* has been
anthologized there is no extended study of the text in its historical context;
by offering something towards such a study I hope to bring out more clearly
the necessity of reading it in conjunction with discussions of Trinitarian
theology elsewhere in Gregory's corpus.

Let me also anticipate my conclusions by noting that in *On Not Three Gods*,
as elsewhere (including the frequently cited *Ad Petrum*—if it is Gregory's),
Gregory makes no extended attempt—and rarely any attempt—to explain

what the divine *prosopa* or *hypostases* are by attributing to each the sorts of mental and psychological characteristics we use to define a distinct human person. Thus, we must also be careful what we think we see in those passages where Gregory does offer some parallels between the divine *hypostases* and three people—how and for what purpose are "social" analogies being used? Often (as in *On Not Three Gods*) Gregory's interest is only in exploring parallel or different logics of differentiation. Indeed, although this question will not receive any extended discussion here, it is noticeable that where we do find Gregory applying psychological categories to the Trinity we often find him happily doing so with reference to the Godhead as analogous to *one* person, the Father's constitution of the Triune Godhead being treated as analogous to one who speaks an intelligible word on his breath or spirit (*Catechetical Oration* 1–2 is paradigmatic here). In fact, in such places Gregory is sometimes willing to apply these categories both to God as one and to the individual persons: the living God speaks an intelligible word as do we, the word possesses its own will as do all living things (although his understanding of "will" for instance requires locating in a very careful historical context). But even here, it is noticeable that we find almost no direct discussion of the interactions between the three divine persons that relies on analogies of interaction between three distinct human agents. Once we realize that analogies with psychological terminologies are not used in the ways modern readings frequently suggest, then perhaps it becomes even clearer that we need to look in more detail at the suppositions of and foundations for Gregory's actual usage.

II: The Polemical Context of On Not Three Gods

It is important first to get a sense of the polemical charge that Gregory faces, and thus the task he sees himself facing if he is to refute his opponents. This charge is that Gregory's theology (and Cappadocian theology more widely[5]) implies the existence of "three Gods" because it was susceptible to the logical analogy of three people. That there is a polemical context for the discussion of this analogy in this text, and that many implications of such an analogy are felt as unacceptable to pro-Nicenes, is clear.[6] Gregory talks initially of Ablabius bringing forward charges made by "opponents of the truth", and elsewhere in the text he refers to those whose charges Ablabius brings forward as "adversaries". It is these "opponents of the truth" who have deployed the analogy of three people to show what they take to be a logical implication of Cappadocian theology. Gregory's opponents are alleging that the relationship between substance and person deployed by the Cappadocians is susceptible to the logic that applies in the case of three people. If so, their charge runs, just as the degree of individuation involved permits us to speak of three "men", the same logic shows us that the Cappadocians are teaching that there are three Gods. It does not seem that Ablabius is himself sympathetic towards the accusation, rather he seems to have been unable to answer their charge to his own satisfaction and has requested help. We need to be clear even here that the opponents in question are not asking whether or not Gregory thinks the divine persons are like three human persons in communion, they are interested only in the degree of individuation the analogy might seem to reveal in Cappadocian Trinitarianism.[7]

The charge that Gregory faces most immediately originates with the problematically named "Macedonians", that is, with those who, most actively during the 360s to 380s, objected to the pro-Nicene inclusion of the Spirit within the Godhead.[8] The Macedonians or "Pneumatomachoi" were a loose group who seem to have accepted the divinity of the Son but were unhappy about the extension of this theology to include the Spirit. They were less a concerted "party" than what Richard Hanson more accurately describes as a diverse "protest movement", arguing against a particular theological move, but coming to that particular oppositional stance from a variety of backgrounds. The detailed structure and belief of those who are to be included in this group does not concern us here, but understanding this polemical context will be very helpful in understanding the direction of Gregory's argument. Accordingly, I will rehearse two pieces of the evidence that demonstrates the origin of the charge and the character of the dispute with which we are concerned.

The text of *On Not Three Gods* itself does not provide us with many clues as to the origin of the charge. However, in Gregory's *Refutation of Eunomius's Confession*, Gregory speaks of "those who keep repeating against us the phrase 'three Gods'."[9] Interestingly, Gregory does not here seem to be referring to Eunomius. Gregory is in the middle of a long exposition of Eunomius's text, an exposition in which he frequently speaks of Eunomius by name, or at least in the singular. At this point in the course of his treatment he offers an extended account of the Spirit's divinity. Gregory attempts to show that the traditional attribution of the work of sanctification to the Spirit alone is mistaken, and that such activity is that of the whole Trinity together. Then begins the short discussion of the anonymous group who charge that Gregory teaches "three Gods". Such people—and suddenly Gregory speaks of his adversaries in the plural—would only have a point if it were first true that pro-Nicenes taught that God was a duality to which we then discussed whether another should be added. However, God is always and by definition one, even though we confess the names of Father, Son and Spirit. Gregory then says that it is time to *resume* his refutation of Eunomius's text. In this short passage Gregory seems clearly to indicate that the charge originates with those who, despite a willingness to accept the divinity of the Son, doubt the divinity of the Spirit and, thus, seem not yet to have grasped the essential unity of the Godhead as pro-Nicene theology has come to present it.

The character of the debate is further revealed by references elsewhere in the Cappadocians. Most directly, at *Oration* 31:13–15, Gregory of Nazianzen attempts to argue against those who say that if the term "God" may be used three times of Father, Son and Spirit then are there not a plurality of powers and hence a plurality of Gods? Nazianzen carefully identifies this charge as originating primarily with those who are "fairly sound" on the Son but who doubt the Spirit's divinity. He even tells us that such people press their charge by alleging that the unity of the pro-Nicene Trinity fails because it is *only* equivalent to the unity of three people. Nazianzen's reply is too complex to explore at length here, but it will be helpful to set it out in summary form. Gregory argues that those who worship the Father and the Son but not the Spirit (his opponents) might be accused of ditheism. Of course, Gregory continues, if they were, then they could only respond by articulating an understanding of Father and Son as *together* constituting the one God whom Christians should worship. In effect their response would be to articulate an account of divinity in which unity is not disrupted by the distinctions of the *hypostases*. Thus, Nazianzen argues, the response of such people against those who might accuse them of ditheism is structurally identical to the response that these people should expect from those who worship Father, Son *and* Spirit: acknowledging commonality of substance does not necessarily involve admitting that the substance itself is divided. Thus there are not three Gods, and the analogy of three people does not apply. Even from this brief summary of Gregory's argument it is clear that the point at issue concerns the very "grammar" of divinity itself.[10]

To understand what I mean by the "grammar" of divinity being at issue we need to note that the fourth century controversies are, in part, easily misunderstood if they are conceived as concentrating on the question "is the Son (and the Spirit) divine?"—some then answering "no" while the "orthodox" simply answer "yes".[11] In this simple form the question already seems to presuppose a complex understanding of "divinity" that implies, for example, no possibility of degrees of divinity; in fact, dispute over the significance of the term and over the rules for talking about divinity was a constant (if sometimes hidden) factor in the debates. To understand the complexity of the questions involved here, it is more helpful to formulate the question offered in the first sentence of this paragraph in exegetical terms as "how can we speak of the Son as being 'one' with the Father (John 10:30; cf. John 1:3) and as being the 'power and wisdom of God' (1 Cor. 1:24), while still asserting that the 'King of kings and Lord of lords alone has immortality and dwells in unapproachable light' (1 Tim. 6:16)?" In different measure anti-Nicene theologians took 1 Tim. 6:16 (and like verses) to be hermeneutically determinative and argued that too close a metaphysical association of the Father and the Son was exegetically mistaken.[12] The simplicity and uniqueness of the Father just would not fit with any direct assertions that Father and Son were truly of the *same* nature. Of course, these exegetical presuppositions demanded of such theologians that they set out an understanding of the relationship between Word, Father and creation that would support this insistence while still being attentive to scriptural material which might seem to point in other directions. In part these questions were answered by subtle, if somewhat *ad hoc*, accounts of degrees of divinity or of hierarchy within the Godhead combined with a strong insistence on the distinct *hypostases* of the persons.[13] Such language stemmed in large part from Origen's account and forms a background not simply for directly anti-Nicene thinkers, but for some whose theology seems in retrospect much closer to later "Nicene" thought. Thus these non- (and in some cases pre-) Nicene theologians possessed a series of implicit rules (a "grammar") for talking about divinity in which the possibility of different degrees of subordinate divinity was combined with an insistence that "true" divinity was simple and indivisible. This grammar provided for a flexible, detailed and persistent exegetical practice.

However, central to the "pro-Nicene" theology which developed in the latter decades of the fourth century was, on the one hand, an insistence that divinity *by definition* is unique and indivisible and, on the other hand, that the distinction between Creator and creation is an absolute one with no mediating degrees or stages.[14] There was also an insistence that the combination of these themes provided the context for discussing the relationship between Father, Son and Spirit: all verses which seemed to indicate any commonality of existence between Father and Son could, in this context, only be taken to indicate the sharing of unique, simple and indivisible divinity.[15] On the other hand, the skill of those theologians who determined the final shape of pro-Nicene theologies was to insist not only on the uniqueness and simplicity of the divine (which could so easily just have resulted in some form of modalist theology), but also on the importance and possibility of according eternal and yet non-materialistic or non-emanationist significance to the language of distinction, relationship and origination that is so central to the Scriptural accounts of the Son's nature. In other words, the tradition of strongly differentiating the *hypostases* and insisting on the importance of defining the Son and Spirit by their relations of origin was incorporated into a changed grammar of divinity which allowed *a priori* for no divine hierarchy or subordination. Origen's understanding of a *hypostasis* as an eternally distinct entity now finds a new home within a subtly but importantly different grammar of divinity. Thus, both Basil and Gregory insist strongly that the persons have "real" existence as individual *hypostases*, but they insist that the grammar of simple and indivisible divinity is the context for all talk of differentiation: it is this combination that marks the real if subtle advance of pro-Nicene theology.[16] Only against the background of this broad shift in the "grammar of divinity" can we understand what it meant for pro-Nicene theologians to talk of the Son being *homoousios* with Father or as "sharing" the divine essence.[17]

However, not only is understanding this theological shift essential to understanding pro-Nicene thought, it is also at this point that pro-Nicene theology was most easily misunderstood. The conflict over the Spirit's divinity reflects both the complexities of resolving the fourth century controversies and the degree to which pro-Nicene theology could be misunderstood. As is clear from the two texts by Nyssa and Nazianzen discussed briefly above, while Macedonian polemic was concerned with the question of the Spirit's divinity, at a deep structural level the Macedonians were also resisting, or not yet grasping, the basic grammar of the Pro-Nicenes' understanding of divinity.

Thus, noting that the charge probably comes from Macedonian circles helps us to see the task that Gregory faces in *On Not Three Gods*. The problem that he faces is not most fundamentally one of explaining how the Spirit is also divine, where both sides in the dispute share a common account of divinity and of the nature of the union between Father and Son. Rather, it is the very character of divine being and unity that is at issue. From *On Not Three Gods* it seems that, while Gregory considers questions of terminological distinction between *ousia, phusis, hypostasis* or *prosopon* to be important, he understands the primary task for an orthodox Trinitarian theologian to be one of setting out an account of theological language and of the divine nature within which one can appropriately deploy the terms on which one settles and within which one can talk the Scriptural language of the Son and the Spirit coming from the Father and acting in the creation.[18]

III: The Structure of On Not Three Gods

We are now in a better position to understand Gregory's intentions in *On Not Three Gods*, and in the following sections I will offer a sequential reading of the text as a whole. In each of these sections my procedure will be to place the arguments of the text in the wider context of other relevant discussions in Gregory's corpus. Looking at the text in this way will help to show how Gregory not only fights on a number of polemical fronts simultaneously, but also how his general strategy is to shift the battle on to ground he has already made his own and away from just skirmishing around the division of universal and particular terminologies.

The text is short but surprisingly complex and a summary of the argument at this stage may be helpful.

At the beginning Gregory introduces the problem and almost immediately tells Ablabius that those who have raised this charge have failed to distinguish between strict linguistic use (in which natures are indivisible and that human nature is not divided between three human beings) and common usage (in which we use the phrase "three men" as if the nature of "man" could be divided). Because, strictly speaking, natures are indivisible, speaking about three *hypostases* does not imply the existence of "three Gods" because the nature of divinity cannot actually be divided. Having given this answer Gregory admits that this is unlikely to be sufficient, given the persistence of the common usage.

Progress, he tells us, can only be made by exploring the name "God-head". Gregory then goes on to argue that names for the divine nature do not describe God directly, but each one describes the action of God: the divine nature remains unknown. "Godhead" itself (*theotes*) stems from our observation of God's act of watching over, seeing or beholding (*thea*), and in our observation of this action we see all three persons engaged in the same action. If their action is one then the power which gives rise to that action is one, and the divine nature itself, although unknown, must be one (Gregory's argument here invokes a technical philosophical terminology for talking about God's nature, power and activity).

At this point, around halfway through the text, Gregory admits that the argument is not yet sufficient because, in created natures, we often see things involved in common operations that are appropriately spoken of as three: three orators or farmers, for instance. Gregory then argues at some length that the action of the three divine persons is shown to be one action not three distinct but similar actions and that, hence, the power that originates them must also be one. The one divine power is constituted by Father, Son and Spirit fulfilling their roles in every unitary divine action. The divine nature and power is thus shown to be undivided. Towards the end of the text Gregory tells us that, even if the main argument he has pursued is not accepted, his first argument was by itself sufficient. Gregory concludes by telling us that all divine attributes should be spoken of in the singular and that the persons may be differentiated by us only according to their causal relationships.

I suggest that this text offers two main arguments: the first takes up directly the charge reported to Gregory by Ablabius and argues simply that natures are strictly indivisible; the second attempts to show that the charge has no force when placed in the context of an appropriate theology of the divine action and power. It is the second argument that most directly gets us to the heart of Gregory's Trinitarian theology. On this basis we can divide up the structure of the text by identifying how Gregory interweaves these two discussions. In the following diagram, the letters A and B indicate the two basic lines of argument I take Gregory to be pursuing, while the Arabic numerals indicate the different stages of those individual arguments through the course of the text:

A.1 We do not speak of three Gods because natures are not divisible: even "three men" is a loose and misleading usage.
  B.1 Natures and their intrinsic powers are known by the operations of those powers, and the divine operation is always observed to be one. Therefore the divine power and nature is indivisibly one.

Question: but surely this doesn't really solve the problem? Three people performing the same operation are still distinct: for example, three people speaking in court are correctly called three orators.

> B.2 True, but operations reveal also the ways in which natures and powers are individuated, and the divine nature is seen to be always one, with a threefold order, and not to be individuated in the same as individual people relate to their common substance.
> A.2 Anyway, as we have already asserted, natures are not divisible.

Conclusion: The combination of B.1 and B.2 best supports our speech about both appropriate unity and appropriate distinction.

My argument will be that, while A.1 and A.2 take up most directly the charge that has been referred to Gregory, it is B.1 and B.2 (arguments originally developed through his controversy with Eunomius) that constitute the argument Gregory thinks conclusive and which we should treat as fundamental in his Trinitarian theology. These two threads of argument (A and B) are related and yet fundamentally distinct. In the following two sections I examine them in turn.

IV: Argument A: Creation and the Indivisibility of Natures

The first and last sections of the argument pursue the strategy that has received most attention in the meager scholarship on this letter.[19] At the beginning of the text Gregory argues that the everyday usage of "three men' to designate three instances of the generic "man" is technically mistaken (A.1). This is so because each "nature" (*phusis*) is uncompound and we should not allow common usage in serious philosophical argument. Indeed, says Gregory, we would run a great danger if we were to transfer such patterns of speech to God: for we know without doubt that God is one. This is so, continues Gregory, "even though the name of Godhead extends through the Holy Trinity". Gregory then uses this comment as a point of departure for turning to the first main section of the text, which considers the meaning of "Godhead" and the nature of theological language (B.1).[20] Towards the end of *On Not Three Gods* Gregory returns again to his opening argument (A.2). Once again Gregory tells us that "natures" are in themselves free from accidents and indivisible. Those whose charge has made its way to Gregory through Ablabius have failed to see that talk of the divine persons being distinct "Gods" as three human beings are three "men" is simply illogical given the character of the universal term "man" and the indivisibility of natures.

It is important to note that Gregory's argument in these sections of the text (A.1 & 2), whether or not it reveals a flawed confusion of logic and ontology to modern eyes, is not concerned with deriving an analogy from the interrelatedness of human community. The argument he offers rests *not* on an account specifically of human nature (let alone of human "community"), but on an ontological or cosmological conception of natures in general. This much is apparent when a similar statement about the indivisibility of natures occurs *en passant* at *Contra Eunomium* III, 4. There Gregory considers the parallel between, on the one hand, the generation of the Son by the Father and, on the other hand, the relationship between the moisture in the grape on the vine and the moisture in wine. Gregory's argument focuses on what is involved in describing wine as a product of the vine. This is an appropriate description, Gregory argues, because there is true community of nature between the grape and the wine: the moisture found in the unpicked grape is essentially the same as that found in the wine.[21] Gregory here offers logically the same argument, and he does so without any need to offer the particular example of three people sharing a common nature. Understanding the place of indivisible natures in Gregory's thought will eventually help us understand many aspects of his argument in *On Not Three Gods*.

The same account of indivisible natures can be found at the heart of his homilies on the first days of creation, the *Hexameron*, and the discussion here begins to reveal to us the reason that the same account is so important throughout *On Not Three Gods*. Although Gregory only deploys one aspect of his understanding of natures (that they are indivisible) in his first argument (A.1–2), other aspects of the same account are central to the rest of the text (B.1–2), and hence a short diversion at this point will eventually pay dividends. In his *Hexameron* homilies Gregory insists that things may be changed from one nature into another, but that natures in themselves are fixed in the act of creation and are indivisible. He writes,

> in the generation of countless animals we see differences according to types and bring them into general harmony by remarking that each one of them is "exceedingly" good ... each one by itself has a perfect nature. A horse is certainly not a cow; the nature and properties of each is conserved, not by a corruption of nature but by the power of their conservation.[22]

Here Gregory deploys an understanding of the "power" (*dunamis*) inherent in each nature to explain their indivisibility: the creation is an act of God's power and follows an ordered sequence in which God, after creating dark unformed matter, endows the dark matter with the light and fire of his own power. Then, through the delegated action of this power which has been given in the act of creation, individual natures come into being. The Word's activity in creation appears here to be the infusion of a power into the creation which, in line with God's will, and mirroring the divine power, diversifies into a variety of distinct and unitary natures each with its own "natural, divinely endowed power". My presentation here simplifies a very complex text, but it does highlight the close links Gregory sees between natures and their intrinsic powers as well as between the indivisibility of natures and God's ordering of creation. A nature has and expresses one intrinsic power: it is hence neither arbitrary nor divisible.

Thus, Gregory's insistence that natures are indivisible is a cosmological doctrine (although, as we shall see, one in turn shaped by his pro-Nicene concerns). For Gregory this account is necessary both for human knowledge of God to be possible, and for understanding the creation's dependence on and autonomy from the Creator. Because natures are the basic principles in which God contemplated the creation, they are indivisible. If they were divisible, then our contemplation could not provide knowledge of God's created activity and hence of God. As I explained above, in the first section of *On Not Three Gods* Gregory deploys only one of the most basic aspects of his account of natures, that they are by definition inseparable. However, in later sections of the argument Gregory uses the same understanding to build a more subtle refutation of the charge with which he is concerned. To those later sections we should now turn. As we leave this section of *On Not Three Gods*, it is important to note that I have not considered in detail how Gregory understands this indivisibility to apply in the particular case of human beings. The character of the individuation among human beings that Gregory envisages here has received a good deal of treatment in the scholarship (and is an extremely complex question[23]). However, I have not dwelt on it here simply because Gregory quickly moves on from this particular argument to what I am arguing is the main theme of his text.

V: Argument B: Natures, Powers, Activities and Knowledge

… whosoever searches the whole of revelation will find therein no doctrine of the Divine nature, nor indeed of anything else that has a substantial existence, so that we pass our lives in ignorance of much, being ignorant first of all of ourselves as men, and then of all things besides. For who is there who has arrived at a comprehension of his own soul?[24]

We can now move on to the middle, and, I suggest, main section of Gregory's argument in *On Not Three Gods* (B.1–2). This main section begins when Gregory insists that we cannot allow loose and misleading patterns of human speech—such as speaking as if human nature could be truly divided—to be transferred to the Godhead and that we can best clear up the charge he faces here by considering the nature of "Godhead" itself. This main section of the text may itself be divided into two related discussions separated by a short interlude.

The first discussion in this main section of the text (B.1) introduces the idea that terms used to describe God do not actually describe God's nature or essence, rather they describe things "around" (*peri*) the divine nature, things through which the divine nature may be known.[25] In a similar vein Gregory says that such divine names enable the investigation of our ideas of the divine, but do not directly signify the divine nature. Gregory goes on to add the idea that all the terms human beings use for God work by creating a special or particular sense (*idian dianoian*). This particular sense takes as its point of departure some feature of our world that reflects the activity of God, and then negates or intensifies that core significance in the attempt to speak worthily of God. In so doing these terms do indicate something that may appropriately be thought or spoken of the divine, but they do not "reach" the divine nature. For example, calling God "giver of life" draws our attention to what is given, not directly to the nature of the giver. With these moves Gregory begins to outline an ontological and epistemological foundation for theological language. In this account of divine naming Gregory follows a course very similar to that set out by Basil and further developed in his own anti-Eunomian polemic. For both Gregory and Basil clarity on this point serves to identify a key difference between Eunomius and the Cappadocians: no term, not even any Scriptural term (let alone a term such as "unbegotten") can be understood to signify the divine nature directly.[26]

The character of human language about God is elsewhere in his corpus frequently discussed by deploying the terminology of *epinoia* (and in the passage of *On Not Three Gods* just discussed *idian dianoian* functions as a synonym for *epinoia*).[27] For Gregory we do not perceive God directly. Rather, as God is unknown to direct human perception we make use of the mental act of *epinoia*, which we can perhaps gloss as "abstracted conception". By *epinoia*—a process more conscious and reflective than might be indicated by such English words as "intuition" or even "perception" in some of its senses —we reflect on things, actions, events and words to break them down into their constituent parts or assumptions. From this act of mental dissection we may come more accurately to focus our thoughts on the event or object under consideration, we move towards acquiring a sense of an object that remains hidden from direct perception. We call God "Giver of Life" and by abstraction we term God "Life"; by reading of God's act of creating all things we learn to speak of God as uncreated. This mode of "knowing" God is, for Gregory, that most fitted to our weak human capacity. Thus by reflection on what Scripture relates to us about divine action we may slowly build up a series of terms, conceptions (*epinoiai*), which we think it appropriate to apply to God—and which are licensed by God's self-revelation in creation and in Scripture—even while we know that in a fundamental sense God remains always unknown. There may be progress in the discipline of *epinoia*, but the hidden and infinite goal of one's practice is never finally achieved. This terminology thus provides one of the most basic contexts for making sense of Gregory's dual insistence that we know something of God, we somehow just manage to "touch" God with the understanding, and yet that God remains always unknown.

For Gregory it is vital that one builds up one's set of appellations for God in a way that preserves appropriate reverence and an appropriate sense of reserve: participating in the established practice of those who already undertake this discipline and sharing their assumptions about what may be reverently said of God is a prerequisite for the good use of *epinoia*. The process of *epinoia* is thus circular (but at its best virtuously so), each act of abstraction needing to enhance, change, and yet stay in conformity with the whole of one's set of appellations for God. Thus Gregory understands the good practice of *epinoia* to be part of a spiritual process, an *askesis* of heart and mind. God's activities and the text of Scripture enable a process of *epinoia* by which we can speak of the divine being, but, Gregory writes, "in applying such appellations to the divine essence, 'which passes all understanding', we do not seek to glory in it by the names we employ, but to guide our own selves by the aid of such terms towards the comprehension of the things which are hidden".[28] In other words, Gregory envisions the process of *epinoia* as part of an on-going shaping of our attention to and speech about something that, more austerely than many commentators would have us imagine, remains always unknown and beyond our grasp. The mind that undertakes this *askesis* does not grasp its object, but is drawn towards the contemplative goal of Christian life.[29] Although this terminology is not a central part of *On Not Three Gods*, the conception of knowledge of God it embodies is central throughout Gregory's corpus and we see its echoes clearly in this text.

However, to understand the main argument of *On Not Three Gods*, to which Gregory is beginning to turn here, we need also to note two aspects of the philosophical traditions from which Gregory draws his nature and power terminology. First, the important link between natures and intrinsic powers in Gregory's cosmology is of great importance for his Trinitarian theology and in his account of human knowledge of God. In a book and two very helpful recent articles, Michel Barnes has gone some way to providing us with the key elements we need to understand Gregory's arguments here. In the first article Barnes has set out the differing traditions of "transcendental causality" that are operative in Gregory and Eunomius's account of the relations between the three divine persons. In Gregory, we find a strong adherence to the idea that the divine nature is inherently productive. One of the fundamental ways in which this is expressed is through the doctrine that the unitary and simple divine power is intrinsic to the indivisible divine nature. Gregory of course insists that such natural productivity and expression is willed not necessary, but his account makes a great deal of use of natural metaphors, such as the fundamental example of a fire and its heat, to emphasize the reality of the ontological union between a nature and its power (a union we have already seen in Gregory's *Hexameron*). In offering this model of "transcendent causality" Gregory demonstrates his debts to a long philosophical and medical tradition which intimately associates the nature or reality of an existent and its power. Gregory's most immediate "intellectual precedent and authority" (to use Barnes' words) for the deployment of this tradition of power terminology in a transcendent context is Plotinus, especially as evident in *Ennead* V.4 (the ancient traditions of medical writing are also important in developing the terminology with which we are concerned here).[30]

In Gregory's account of how theological language reaches only what is "around" the Godhead, and in his account of God's ordering of creation in terms of natures and powers, we see him making use of another facet of this philosophical tradition. Indeed, Gregory again seems to be following Plotinus's lead: both writers not only talk of a power as being intrinsic to a nature, but also metaphorically present a power as being "around" a nature. In *Ennead* V.1, a text which makes a frequent appearance in Cappadocian theology, Plotinus describes the power that each thing exhibits as "a surrounding reality directed to what is outside".[31] In *Ennead* V.4 Plotinus uses this very same language about both *nous* and *psyche* to indicate how their generative nature expresses itself in creation. Here, the talk of powers being "around' natures serves as a way of indicating that although powers are the cause of the activity of *nous* and *psyche* outside themselves, the natures themselves remain somehow unknown and distinct.[32] Similarly Gregory too speaks of theological language as reaching that which is "around" the divine nature, that is, the divine nature's power which gives rise to divine activity in the world. This metaphorically spatial language nicely indicates the distinction between knowing the power of a nature and knowing a nature directly, and is often reinforced, as at *Ennead* V.1, by means of the analogy of the sun and its rays. In both Gregory and Plotinus we know the rays but not directly the sun: in Gregory we may grow in knowledge of the divine power through its operations even while the divine nature remains unknown.

However, and second, Gregory talks not only of nature and power, but also of activity (*energeia*), and here we come to the second article by Michel Barnes to which I wish to draw attention. In distinguishing these three terms Gregory is employing a technical sequence of causal language in which, as we have seen, a nature has an intrinsic power which contains or expresses the causal capacity of a nature whether or not it is actually operative.[33] Activities *ad extra* are set in motion by a nature's power and it is by observing activities that we may reason back to the character of the power that is operative. In *On Not Three Gods* Gregory hints at the connection between, on the one hand, natures and their intrinsic powers (a connection which he elsewhere draws out more fully), and he also very clearly links, on the other hand, activities with the powers that they reveal. For example, Gregory speaks of "the various activities of the transcendent power" through which the power is known directly after he has indicated that natures remain unknowable except through activities.[34] At this point nature seems almost interchangeable with power, an interchangeability best explained by placing the reference in the context of the causal sequence discussed here.

While it is, I think, a mistake to paint Gregory too quickly as the architect of an unprecedented and revolutionary theological ontology, Gregory's theology incorporates ontological and cosmological doctrines into a complex system of thought which provides the constant foundation for his articulation of pro-Nicene Trinitarian theology. It is also important to note the flexibility of the traditions with which Gregory is here engaged. The flexibility of this language is a key point in its favor when it is being used not only to describe the character of created reality, but also to shape and provide an account of the Creator, who is conceived as both creating a world in His own image and yet as being truly distinct from it. Thus, when it suits his purpose Gregory deploys different aspects of nature, power and activity terminology in an attempt to characterize human knowledge and speech of God. We must watch carefully to spot the allusions that Gregory makes to this terminology, but we should beware of mistaking his complex and *ad hoc* allusion for simple incoherence. It is time now to return to the course of the first main section of the argument (B.1).

Having insisted that we know only the power of a thing not its nature, Gregory goes on to argue that "Godhead" (*theotes*) is itself a term which originates in observation of the divine activity of seeing or contemplating. Gregory asserts that the name "Godhead" has originated from observing that God sees and comprehends all. However, Father, Son and Spirit all seem to be engaged in the *same* activity of seeing and contemplating. Thus, says Gregory, if the activities are the same, then the power which gave rise to them is the same and the ineffable divine nature in which that power is inherent must also be one.[35] There is, then, no basis on which to speak of a divided divine nature, because the divine operation that has given rise to our conception of Godhead itself is not divided. If the operation is one, then the power that gave rise to that operation must be one. The divine nature remains unknown but its power is revealed to be one.[36] Gregory has thus offered a refutation of the charge that his teaching implies three Gods, but one considerably more sophisticated than his first attempt (in section A.1) concentrating solely on the logic of differentiation. However, the force of this second refutation will only be felt by someone who first accepts the significance of knowledge following observation of activity and then accepts Gregory's account of how divine activity is described in Scripture.

Gregory's intention seems to be one of showing that the "three Gods" charge is best faced by opening a discussion about two fundamental questions: what do we mean by "divine nature"?; how it is possible for us to speak of divine nature? As Gregory knows well, these two questions are inseparable: he sets up a foundation for our speaking of God, but only by also beginning to offer an account of the divine nature and its activity. The epistemological question must receive an ontological and a cosmological answer, but the cosmology is already shaped by a consideration of how God creates and of how the creation imitates that divine nature. Of course, Gregory's answers to these questions already also contain an answer to the question of whether the divine nature can be divided. Nevertheless, his purpose should not be understood solely as one of fixing the cards so that the "Macedonian" will lose. Rather, we should understand him as indicating that questions about the divine nature can only be faced once one has in place appropriate conceptions of the relations between Creator and creation and of the character of human knowledge of God. In other words, articulating the pro-Nicene grammar of divinity (as with all grammars of divinity) necessarily involves articulating an account of the relationship between Creator and creation. Major arguments *in* Trinitarian theology can only be conducted by also arguing about the character *of* Trinitarian theology. Such an argument involves deploying cosmological and epistemological principles within which we may come to understand the texture of theological language. We will return to the significance of Gregory's attempt to answer the specific question he faces by raising these more general questions later: for the moment I want to return to the course of his argument.

Having introduced the text's central argument, Gregory now offers a rhetorically sophisticated short interlude, admitting that his main argument seems so far to have offered no reason why we should not speak of three Gods.[37] In fact, he argues, the attempt to argue only from the nature of operations or activities might seem to make pro-Nicene theology even more susceptible to the charge that has been raised. This is so because there seem to be plenty of cases where we admit common operation but are also clear that distinct individuals are involved. Thus, for example, we speak of many orators or farmers purely on the basis of common operation and without reference to a shared nature at all. On the other hand, says Gregory in a quick aside, if we *did* suppose that we could actually know the divine nature, then the observation of the unified divine action in creation would seem to emphasize the importance of subsuming the persons under a unitary Godhead. But, he continues, since that course is forbidden to us because we want to argue only from operations, it really does seem that the argument so far has only strengthened the case of those who want to say that pro-Nicene theology implies three Gods. The interlude ends by Gregory saying that he has tried to highlight the possible response of his adversaries so that the direction of his argument may be clearer.

This short passage of *On Not Three Gods* serves a number of purposes. On the one hand, it cleverly serves to put off the charge that the question actually posed is simply not being faced; on the other hand, it serves to highlight what has so far been missing from Gregory's account. While he has indicated the importance of distinguishing nature and operations as the referent of theological language, and while he has indicated the unity of the persons in their activity, Gregory has not yet offered a fully convincing account of the link between the common actions of the divine persons and the indivisibility of the divine nature that he sees as central to pro-Nicene theology. That answer comes in the second half of the work's main section (B.2) where Gregory offers a more extensive account of the link between inner-divine causality and operation *ad extra*.

After this interlude, then, Gregory resumes his main argument (B.2). His next step is to indicate the distinction between the inseparable union of the divine persons in their activity and the accidental or coincidental activity of human persons undertaking some common project or business. Different human persons may undertake the same task but they do not directly participate in the action of others and each one possesses his or her own special sphere of activity.[38] In other terms, terms hinted at here but developed in more detail in the *Ad Graecos*, the actions of human beings demonstrate an interrelated causal matrix which reveals human beings to have a substance that may be individuated in a way characteristic of the created order. Not only do individual persons possess their own activity, they also reveal themselves to be impermanent and to be caused by previous generations of human beings.[39] Operations thus reveal the character of the powers and natures with which they are connected. However, in the case of the Father we find no activity in which the Son does not also work. Similarly, the Son has no "special activity" without the Spirit. The point is a fairly subtle one: whatever sort of individuality and difference exists between the three divine persons it is not the sort of individuality we observe in an existent that has its own self-caused and distinct activity.

The divine persons, thus, do not simply act together, they function inseparably to constitute any and every divine activity towards the creation. Gregory goes on to articulate his position further by developing his account of inner divine causality. He talks of the power or action of God "issuing from the Father as from a spring, [being] brought into operation by the Son, and perfecting its grace by the power of the Spirit".[40] This phrase, and others like it, have sometimes been taken to indicate the "personal" character of Gregory's Trinitarian theology, as if Gregory were telling us that the divine persons co-operated, at the Father's initiative, to bring to fruition every divine action. Unfortunately, although such a reading correctly highlights the position of the Father in this sequence, such a reading also misses key elements of Gregory's argument. Gregory, of course, does not want to deny that the divine persons possess their own distinct and irreducible hypostatic existence. However, his account of divine action uses a philosophical model of causality to present the three not as possessing distinct actions towards a common goal, but as together constituting *just one distinct action* (because they are one power). Gregory here makes no attempt to apply psychological categories to explain what it means for the persons to be distinct within the unitary divine power and deploys no language that obviously relies on metaphors of co-operation.[41]

On the basis of this argument Gregory can now present his second answer to the critique of pro-Nicene theology in a more sophisticated and powerful form. The activity of divine persons, as seen in creation and described in Scripture, is of a character that shows God's power (and hence the divine nature) not to be individuated as is human nature. Here it may help to call to mind some aspects of Gregory's theology that are only partially alluded to in *On Not Three Gods*: God has created a world whose order and structure is (at infinite remove) a reflection of God's own power.[42] Because God has created the world in this way, the logic of power and activity that we see in God's creation should reveal to us something of God's activity and power.[43] On this basis Gregory can assert that through observing God's activity—which should be seen in creation and is narrated in Scripture—we can see that God's one power works always by a unitary causal sequenced activity of the three persons. The divine action does not reveal to us individuated natures parallel to those revealed by human activity. The divine action or will is the will of the Father that proceeds through the Son to the Spirit, and yet without that will being only the action of the Father, nor being the action of three together. It is, thus simply inappropriate to speak of three Gods, because we do not observe three distinct actions in the divine activity.

However, this observation does not serve only the purpose of indicating that the three have a unitary power, and a unitary "motion and disposition of the good will",[44] it also serves to emphasize the unique and incomprehensible nature of the divine power. This is so because Gregory does not allow us to argue that what we observe in the divine activity is just one acting power (I hesitate to say "one existent" acting—although this is the analogy on which Gregory relies): the divine power is one, and yet Scripture and the consequent confession of the Church insist that the persons are three. Gregory's ontology *is* intrinsic to his argument, but the argument serves to indicate the uniqueness of the God revealed in the Scriptural account and even something of the character of the ineffability that is the Creator. This last sentence is explored more fully in my conclusion, but it is important to note here that in these themes Gregory provides us with an archetypal example of the context in which he deploys analogical accounts of the divine unity or distinction, and it is only by placing those analogies in this context that we can grasp the degree to which we should rest in any one analogy or even in any particular combination of analogies.

In the final few pages of the text (my section A.2), Gregory both turns back to the initial answer he had given to Ablabius's question based on his understanding of the indivisibility of natures, and offers a few more hints about the importance of grasping the unitary divine causality. That Gregory is willing to revert to his initial argument at this stage—and that he even hints at a third argument which would argue that "Godhead" cannot be the name of a nature because God is above every name—may be taken simply to be evidence of Gregory's willingness to provide Ablabius with a variety of polemical resources. However, one might also argue that in pursuing this multi-pronged tactic Gregory demonstrates a keen awareness of how his theology is attempting to argue for a context to knowledge of God that many of his contemporaries may have found too strongly insistent on the inability of humans to talk of the divine nature. Gregory adds to his argument that natures are by definition indivisible that, while Scripture itself deploys this common convention in a number of places, Scripture never speaks of God in the plural: "The Father is God: the Son is God: and yet, by the same proclamation God is One, because no difference either of nature or of operation is contemplated in the Godhead."[45]

Gregory here also turns to those who might think that his insistence on the unity of the divine nature serves to confuse the distinctions of the persons. It is, he insists, only in the structure of the causal relationships between the persons that we can make any real distinctions. The sequence of the one divine action *ad extra* reflects the nature and order of God's *internal* generation, and in both the same sequence of causality is operative. Nevertheless, this internal structure does not describe the nature of the persons, but their mode of having or exercising that which remains ineffable. Because persons and essence are identical, that in which the persons consist also remains unknown:

> ... when we learn that He is unbegotten, we are taught in what mode he exists, and how it is fit that we should conceive Him as existing, but what He is we do not hear in that phrase.[46]

Gregory's deployment of the language of individuation here (as elsewhere) is notoriously difficult to interpret, and I do not intend to enter that technical discussion in detail. However, it is not usually noted how Gregory's talk of a *hypostasis* having a "manner of existence" is clearly set within his distinction between the unknowability of the divine nature and the knowability of the divine power's operations. The manner of existence is known, the language that we should confess about the divine person is known, but the nature of the person is always unknown. Whether or not Gregory's deployment of this sort of individuation language is at all helpful in itself, it is important to note how his placing of that language in this particular context helps him further to elucidate his account of appropriate human talk of God. We may speak of the way in which a person contributes to the divine activity—and thereby we understand something more of the divine power—but the nature itself remains ineffable. Thus, the language of individuation is itself partly deployed in order to emphasize that the nature of which we speak remains ineffable and hence we may fairly conclude that Gregory thinks that even the manner of individuation itself remains ineffable.

VI: Conclusion

> ... for we, who are initiated into the mystery of godliness by the divinely
> inspired words of the Scripture do not see between the Father and the
> Son a partnership of Godhead, but a unity ...[47]

On Not Three Gods does not offer an account of an analogy between three
human persons and the three divine "persons" dependent on a psychologically dense account of what it is to be a person. The text does not focus
its argument on a particular explanation of the terminology of *ousia* and
hypostasis, and it does not even treat that very particular logic of unity and
differentiation which Gregory understands to exist between three people
as important for Trinitarian theology unless it is understood against the
background of his discussion of the unity of the divine nature, power and
activity. In not doing these various things, and in what it does actually do, I
would argue that this text plays out for us, in a particular polemical context,
the fundamental themes of Gregory's Trinitarian theology.

At the beginning and end of the text Gregory is indeed directly concerned
with whether his account of the Godhead falls prey to the same logic of
differentiation that operates between three people. However, the bulk of *On
Not Three Gods* is taken up with drawing out a related but distinct argument
that does not begin with a particular understanding of differentiation or
individuation in the Godhead (although it does *result* in such an account).
Rather, this main argument of the text begins by establishing an account of
the character of human knowledge of God and an account of the ontological
principles on which our speech of the Trinity should be founded. This
account provides, for Gregory, the necessary background against which
we should offer any account of the logic of differentiation of the divine
hypostases, and against which we should offer any analogy for the character
of their communion. In this light perhaps we should begin to teach and read
Gregory assuming different texts to be paradigmatic. Rather than turning first
to *On Not Three Gods* I suggest we make far more use of three texts: *Catechetical
Oration*, *Refutation of Eunomius' Confession* and *Contra Eunomium* II.[48]

At the end of this rather extended investigation let me set out three
observations about the wider character of Gregory's Trinitarian theology
that follow from my discussion. These three points overlap, but they do so
in treating some of the central themes of this paper as the point of departure
for sketching an agenda for the study of Gregory's Trinitarian theology.

1. Gregory's various deployments of the sequence nature-power-activity,
and his insistence that, while operations reveal their originating powers,
natures remain unknown and ineffable, is the cosmological and ontological
foundation on which his account of Trinitarian theology is built. However,
these reflections deliver not simply Gregory's account of God's ineffability,
but his account of what we might term the *character* of God's ineffability.

In the first of his homilies on *The Song of Songs* Gregory writes in general terms,

> the unlimited [divine] nature cannot be accurately contained by a name; rather, every capacity for concepts, and every form of words and names, even if they seem to contain something great and befitting God's glory, are unable to grasp his reality. But starting from certain traces and sparks, as it were, our words aim at the unknown, and from what we can grasp we make conjectures by a kind of analogy about the ungraspable ... the wonders visible in the universe give material for the theological terms by which we call God wise, powerful, good, holy, blessed, eternal, judge, savior, and so forth ... the human mind is unable to find any description, example, or adequate expression of that beauty ...[49]

In this passage, Gregory's well known insistence on the divine infinity founds a complex account of theological analogy. On the one hand, the creation seems to provide points of departure for our talk of God (and here Gregory should not be thought of as conceiving of creation as a separate source from Scripture: Scriptural narrative and terminology are taken to direct our attention appropriately to the ways in which creation mirrors the divine existence through the presence of delegated power). On the other hand, Gregory insists that God remains at infinite remove from our understanding; the divine creator creates a context in which human beings may move in trust and in truth towards God, but God is not comprehended.

Elsewhere in Gregory's theology, beyond this brief section of his commentary on the *Song of Songs*, we find the logic of natures, powers, and activities enabling a more concrete account of the relationship between the activities we observe and the realities initiating them. But note that Gregory constantly uses his schema to force upon us a deliberate and focused *askesis* of the imagination, insisting that the logic of ineffable natures known through the activity of their intrinsic powers is fundamental to the structure of the creation itself. If we are to make progress in knowledge of God, we must develop appropriate attention to the character of *all* our knowledge. The particular discipline of epistemological reserve and cultivated attention to Scripture (and to the creation in Scripture's light) that Gregory shapes is thus founded on a developed theology of the divine infinity and power and a developed account of the created order and ontological difference.[50] From these themes flows a developing reflection on the very character and "texture" of Christian faith. And thus, for Gregory, careful development of these themes is intrinsic and fundamental to the good practice of Trinitarian theology.

2. In the last sentence of his summary of Gregory's Trinitarian theology Richard Hanson reports, but makes little of, Karl Holl's 1904 description of Gregory's God as a life-imparting power (*zoopoios dunamis*) in three forms.[51]

In fact, Holl's brief account is both extremely perceptive and provides a good basis for discussing the general conception of Gregory's Trinitarian theology that I think shines through the complex argument of *On Not Three Gods*. Holl both saw Gregory's account of the simple and ineffable divine power prefigured in Basil and (to a lesser extent) Gregory Nazianzen, and, in its particular and extensive development, as the theme which distinguished Gregory's account from that of the other "Cappadocian" theologies. For Holl, Gregory makes his own a theme that the other Cappadocians treat as one among many themes. Holl also sees Gregory's vision of what is revealed in—and active in—the scriptural account of salvation history as revolving around the revelation of a three-fold divine power. This theme is the site for Gregory's development of a remarkably complex and fruitful account of the distinction between creation and the distinct, un-mediately present Creator, an account that is fundamental to the whole of his thought world.[52] This account of God as life-imparting power also provides Gregory with the basis for a soteriology which draws together an understanding of God's salvific divine power restoring the creation and a theology of creation in which God has shown himself in creation as the one whose inexhaustible power sustains and exists always in an economy of infinite plenitude. In this theology of redemption Christ's being one with the divine power, being *the* divine power, is the basis for the incorporation of all into the life and power of Christ.[53]

Importantly, Holl also treats Gregory's account of the divine power which *is* the threefold being of Father, Son and Spirit as the point of departure for his brief treatment of the ways in which the persons are differentiated.[54] As I indicated towards the end of the last main section, Gregory's talk of the individuation of the persons is itself not intended to result in one account of the difference between them. Rather he is primarily concerned to give an account of the conditions under which we must speak of difference and the conditions under which we speak of unity. At the same time he seeks to rule out conceptions of either unity or differentiation that he takes to be incompatible with these basic conditions for speech about God. Throughout, the actual mode of the persons' individuation remains hidden from us even as Gregory continually insists that only confession of the reality and eternity of the hypostatic distinctions can do justice to the account of God's activity with which Scripture presents us.

I would, however, argue that Holl fails to follow through on his own logic where he assumes in Gregory the presence of a subtle subordinationism of Son and Spirit, and suggests that he has not sufficiently followed his own logic. This is, however, a large topic, and here I want to draw attention to just two relevant areas of discussion. In the first case, I suggest that the basic logic of the unity of the divine nature and power discussed here should be understood to govern statements about the causal order Gregory sees as distinguishable in the Trinity just as much as it is understood to govern the logic of distinction Gregory describes between the three persons. In the latter case, as I have just suggested, Gregory insists that the distinctions between the persons are real, and yet the mode of existence of the persons as distinct and yet one is beyond our comprehension. Similarly, in the former case, Gregory insists that the order we perceive in Scriptural discussion of the Trinity does not involve spatial or temporal separation or sequence because of the unity and simplicity of the divine existence. Thus, once again, Gregory's account of the divine unity is intended to render inappropriate a whole range of consequences we might see as following any account of divine hierarchy, consequences necessary in created reality. But, just as Gregory's deployment of divine unity serves to render the divine distinctions confessed in faith ultimately incomprehensible (they cannot be understood as identical to the sort of distinctions we observe in *any* created example), so too the same deployment renders ultimately incomprehensible the mode of activity which the Scriptures allow us to narrate as inseparable and as occurring through the Son and being completed in the Spirit.

Of course, even if I am right about the structure of Gregory's argumentation, this does not necessarily mean that there is no hierarchy in Gregory's account. It means that we cannot assume an implicit ontological subordinationism to be present without much further work. It is just such an ontological subordinationism that Holl's account assumed, following the line of interpretation that all "Cappadocian" Trinitarianism was forever marked by Basil's early association with "Homoiousian" theology. Even if this thesis is no longer seen as viable—as the vast majority of recent scholarship has agreed—there may well be some sorts of acceptable hierarchy in our narrations of Trinitarian theology. The priority of the Father—even if it is the priority of one who eternally gives rise to a mutuality of loving exchange—*is* in some sense a priority.

3. As a number of recent studies have argued, Gregory accepts and makes use of a variety of terminologies for describing the relationship between the divine unity and the divine persons; *ousia, phusis, hypostasis* and *prosopon* are all brought into service when it is deemed necessary.[55] The agreement that it was possible to acknowledge three *hypostases* without implying that God was more than one ultimate principle was indeed central to the latter stages of the fourth century controversies. However, as I have shown, Gregory's theology demonstrates that making such a move occurred within a wider reshaping of the very grammar of divinity: Gregory's theology of the infinite and simple divine power is the context within which he can articulate the possibility of eternally distinct *hypostases* within the one divine power. Here I have argued, with reference to *On Not Three Gods*, that Gregory does not himself bring forward the analogy of three people and that he is concerned primarily with the logic of individuation that this analogy implies. Elsewhere in his corpus he consistently discusses the analogy in the same

context, using this analogy to focus on the logical relationships between the Trinitarian persons. This does not mean that psychological categories play no role in his thought, as the paper in this collection by Michel Barnes so well demonstrates. But his use of psychological analogies and the assumptions with which he uses those analogies differ markedly from the concerns of modern "social" Trinitarians.

Some readers will no doubt be puzzled by my lack of discussion of Gregory's short *Ad Graecos* and the text that survives among Basil's corpus as *Letter 38* but which is frequently now assumed to be by Gregory and has become known as the *Ad Petrum*. Again, a few remarks will indicate the directions in which I would wish to push discussion of the place of these texts. First, it is clear in the concluding sections of the *Ad Petrum* that the author insists on the importance of placing any such terminological discussions in the context of an overall account of the relations between Creator and creation and in the context of an account of the divine unity virtually identical to the accounts found in *On Not Three Gods*. Hence, at least one of these texts presents its arguments as needing not just some supplementation but the vital context of the wider themes more strongly apparent elsewhere in Gregory's corpus. Thus arguments built on the concerns of these texts, I would argue, need to be constructed with overt reference to the ways in which they represent the wider corpus of Gregory's Trinitarian writing. Second, the use of the logic of differentiation between three people in those texts is substantially the same as that found in *On Not Three Gods*: the discussion focuses around the logic of differentiation not around the communion shared between three persons understood in psychologically dense terms. Thus, while these texts provide much useful material for the scholar exploring Gregory's understanding of unity and differentiation among human beings, I do not think they could serve as useful introductions to his Trinitarianism as a whole, and in the areas they do cover, the account offered is broadly the same as that found throughout Gregory's corpus.

In *On Not Three Gods* and elsewhere Gregory does tell us, of course, that we can distinguish the persons with causal language. Now, given the structure of modern readings of Gregory, it is only to be expected that mention of this argument will result in the question being posed "what degree of distinction does this causal language involve?" I suspect that the clearest we can come to the answer that Gregory might give to this question is to say "we do not know". Scripture demands that we confess a logic of eternal distinction which insists that insofar as we can talk of God as an eternal and distinct reality, so too we can speak of Father and Son and Spirit as eternally distinct realities. At the same time Scripture demands that we speak of a unitary divine power and nature, *and*, for Gregory, it demands of us analogical talk that attempts to explore the resonances and implications of the character of God's action as narrated in Scripture. For those modern commentators who accept the account of east and west as differentiated by a preference for social or mental analogies, failure to deploy some sort of social analogy of necessity implies a failure to distinguish the three persons appropriately. However, such an equation is not a necessary one and its deployment reveals a lack of understanding of the peculiarly modern preoccupation that makes it seem plausible.

To describe how Gregory does consider that we should analogically talk about the distinction between the persons and their unity, we would need to see how he combines together distinct analogical fields in particular texts, adapting analogical traditions to serve within his overall grammar of the divine and of theological language. Demonstrating how this is so—and thus coming to provide a more detailed answer to particular ways of presenting Gregory's analogical preferences—is the subject for much other work. Indeed, I suggest that such research should be seen as an urgent need in the study of classical Trinitarian theology. However, on the basis of my argument here I can say that in every case we will only read Gregory well if we constantly bear in mind how those analogical discussions are intended to play a part within a particular *askesis* of the soul and of the imagination, and in every case we would need to bear in mind the ontological foundations for such talk. Only if we learn to do this would we really learn, at last, to appreciate Gregory as a pro-Nicene theologian.

NOTES

1 Gregory of Nyssa, *Contra Eunomium* (hereafter CE) II (GNO I/1, 256; NPNF V, 260). Note: all references to works of Gregory are accompanied both by references both to the appropriate GNO volume (where possible) (Gregorii Nysseni Opera, W. Jaeger *et al.*, ed [Leiden: E. J. Brill, 1960ff.]) and to a published English translation (where possible). The most frequently cited translation is that of NPNF (Nicene and Post Nicene Fathers [Edinburgh: T. & T. Clark, 1880ff.]).

2 I would like to thank Michel Barnes, John Behr, Sarah Coakley, Andrew Louth, Medi Ann Volpe and Robert Wilken for their comments on an earlier version of this paper which was read as a "Master Theme" at the Thirteenth International Patrisics Conference, Oxford, August 1999. I also wish to thank the editors of the *Journal of Early Christian Studies*, Profs. Elizabeth Clark and Patout Burns (and two anonymous readers for that journal) for releasing this paper from their publication schedule to appear here.

3 By "pro-Nicene" theologians I refer to those who, from a variety of different but related perspectives, came, in the latter half of the fourth century, to shape theologies which argued *for* a particular interpretation of Nicaea's terminology and which offered a wider theological context for that interpretation. These theologies went on to provide the foundation for the orthodoxy defined in the early 380s. As recent scholarship has increasingly made clear these, theologies share foundational principles across a number of supposed traditional linguistic or geographical divisions. See for examples the literature cited in note 11 and, on western themes, my "'Remember that you are Catholic' (*serm.* 52,2): Augustine on the Unity of the Triune God", *Journal of Early Christian Studies* 8 (2000), pp. 39–82; Michel René Barnes, "Re-reading Augustine's theology of the Trinity", in S. T. Davis, D. Kendall and G. O'Collins (eds), *The Trinity: An Interdisciplinary Symposium on the Doctrine of the Trinity* (Oxford & New York: Oxford University Press, 1999), pp. 56–71.

4 In my *Nicaea and Its Legacy* (Oxford: Oxford University Press, forthcoming), I offer a more extensive (but still brief) discussion of modern readings of Gregory's supposed "pluralism", especially insofar as these readings are an excellent example of the ways in which modern

theological summaries and textbook presentations are often primarily expressions of only half-conscious commitment to late nineteenth century narratives of early Christian doctrine rather than expressions of in-depth engagement with the texts themselves and with on-going scholarship on those texts. Indeed, it is noticeable that Nyssa—or the "Cappadocians" in general—is frequently cited but almost entirely without any detailed attempt at reading his texts. Two exceptions to this rule—whether or not I agree with the result—are Robert Jenson and Cornelius Plantinga.

5   Although in general it is important to distinguish the theologians of Basil and the two Gregorys, here Gregory is encountering a charge first faced by Basil, and now being faced by the two Gregorys. The charge, as I hope to show, goes to the heart of a concern shared by all three thinkers.

6   It is fascinating (but the question must probably remain unanswered in any determinate way) to ask whether we might extend my point about *On Not Three Gods* here and say that even the extended discussions of the analogy between three people and the three divine persons in Cappadocian discussions were stimulated not by their wishing to offer the analogy but by opponents bringing it forward. Of course there is some material in previous tradition—and in the fourth century controversies—that makes *ad hoc* use of such an analogy in some form, but not what precisely stimulated Cappadocian attempts to be precise about the logic of individuality using this parallel. It is not intrinsically connected to the emergence of a careful distinction between *ousia* and *hypostasis*, although those discussions—in Cappadocian theology—do sometimes coincide.

7   An earlier article by Lucian Turcescu demonstrates the problem of discussing Gregory's understanding of "person" with reference to the *Ad Petrum* (previously treated as Basil's *ep.* 38). In "The Concept of Divine Persons in Gregory of Nyssa's *To His Brother Peter, On the Difference Between* Ousia *and* Hypostasis", *Greek Orthodox Theological Review* 42 (1997), pp. 63–82, Turcescu clearly shows that the language of *hypostasis* is not used primarily to identify something which is then filled with individual psychological content, but he then insists, largely on the weak grounds that the hypostases are described with terms that may be translated as "relational" and "perichoretic", that the Cappadocians *do* mean something like a community of persons! Turcescu's essay in this volume seems to pursue the best lines of his earlier article in carefully distinguishing Nyssa's discussion of persons from the concerns of some modern theologians.

8   For a brief outline of the nature of "Macedonian" theology and the problems of using the term see Richard P. C. Hanson, *The Search for the Christian Doctrine of God* (Edinburgh: T. & T. Clark, 1988), pp. 760–772. More extensively see Michael A. G. Haykin, *The Spirit of God: The Exegesis of 1 and 2 Corinthians in the Pneumatomachian Controversy of the Fourth Century* (Leiden: E. J. Brill, 1994), esp. chps. 3, 4 and the very useful bibliography; W.-D. Hauschild, *Die Pneumatomachen. Eine Untersuchung zur Dogmengeschichte des vierten Jahrhunderts*, Diss. University of Hamburg, 1967. Unfortunately Haykin offers no discussion of *On Not Three Gods*, his account focusing primarily on Athanasius's encounter with the *Tropici* and on Basil's pneumatology. I say that the charge "most immediately" originated with this group because, of course, treating Father and Son as co-eternal was viewed as implying two ultimate principles from the earliest stages of the fourth century controversies and before.

9   Gregory of Nyssa, *Refutation of Eunomius's Confession* (hereafter *Ref.*), 14 (GNO II/2, 394–395; NPNF V, 129–130).

10   This account of the polemical context of *On Not Three Gods* may be further reinforced by Basil's insistence at *On the Holy Spirit*, 18, 45 that "we do not say 'one, two, three', or 'first, second, and third'" and by his strong insistence that ranking the Spirit with Father and Son does not mean that the divine nature and power is now threefold. The sections where Basil argues that the three persons are not to be enumerated as if they were divided objects is most likely not to be an abstract treatment of the paradox of number in the Trinity, but a specific response to the sort of polemical charge Gregory faces a few years later.

11   The fourth century Christological and Trinitarian controversies have undergone much reinterpretation in recent decades, and that process of reinterpretation continues. For recent accounts of the latter half of the fourth century and of the significance of Cappadocian Trinitarianism see Michel René Barnes, "The Fourth Century as Trinitarian Canon", in Lewis Ayres & Gareth Jones (eds) *Christian Origins: Theology, Rhetoric and Community* (London & New York: Routledge, 1998), pp. 47–67; André de Halleux, "'Hypostase' et 'Personne' dans

la formation du dogme trinitaire (ca. 375–381)", *Revue d'Histoire Ecclesiastique* 79 (1984), pp. 313–369; 625–670; idem, "Personnalisme ou essentialisme trinitaire chez les Pères cappadociens", *Revue théologique de Louvain* 17 (1986): pp. 129–155; 265–292; Joseph T. Lienhard, "The Arian Controversy: Some Categories Reconsidered," *Theological Studies* 48 (1987), pp. 415–436; idem, "Ousia and hypostasis: the Cappadocian Settlement and the Theology of 'One hypostasis'", in Stephen T. Davis, Daniel Kendall and Gerald O'Collins (eds), *The Trinity: An Interdisciplinary Symposium on the Doctrine of the Trinity* (Oxford & New York: Oxford University Press, 1999). The best introduction to the controversies available in English is currently Basil Studer, *Trinity and Incarnation: The Faith of the Early Church*, trans. Marius Westerhoff, edited by Andrew Louth (Edinburgh: T. & T. Clark, 1993), chps. 9–14. See also my *Nicaea and Its Legacy, passim.*

12　E.g., Arius, *Letter to Alexander*, 2; Eunomius, *Apology*, 21. The appearance of the verse in both these texts should not be taken as evidence of a direct connection between the two, but rather a common interest in an exegetical *topos* that served both their theologies and which had a history extending back beyond its significance in the fourth century.

13　Within such a grammar many moves are possible. Eusebius of Caesarea's *Letter to his Church concerning the Synod at Nicaea* provides ample evidence for the truth of this statement. Eusebius is able to assent to the *homoousion* in some form while still differentiating Father and Son in a basically hierarchical manner. For a very useful introduction to Eusebius's theology, see J. Rebecca Lyman, *Christology and Cosmology: Models of Divine Activity in Origen, Eusebius and Athanasius* (Oxford: Oxford University Press, 1993), pp. 90–99; 106–123.

14　E.g., Gregory of Nyssa, *De Spiritu Sancto* (GNO III/1, 91; NPNF V, 316): "Deity, in fact, exhibits perfection in every line in which the good can be found. If it fails and comes short of perfection in any single point, in that point the conception of deity will be impaired, so that it cannot, therein, be called Deity at all."

15　These themes then served as a key polemical tool against the varieties of subordinationist language deployed by very different anti-Nicene theologians in the latter stages of the controversy.

16　It is because the language of differentiation and relation is incorporated within this revised grammar of the divine that Harnack's old charge that Cappadocian Trinitarianism is "semi-Arian" just misses the point. I return to this point in the conclusion to the paper.

17　One piece of evidence for this view of the shifts involved is the very lack of attention paid to the term *homoousios* by some of the key players in the latter stage of the controversy. See Barnes, "The Fourth Century as Trinitarian Canon", pp. 58–62.

18　Much twentieth century Trinitarianism has taken any text that begins by discussing the "unity" of God to be offering this term as the fundamental point of reference for describing God in a way that serves only to deny the Trinitarian character of the divine for Christians. Some writers have, however, taken a more subtle approach and noted that such discussions actually function to introduce Trinitarian theology by first arguing some basic points about the rules for discussion of divinity (and for the relationship between Creator and creation), rules that are intrinsic to Christian Trinitarianism and which in no way reduce the possibility of articulating a fully Trinitarian perspective (the work of David Burrell on Aquinas is here particularly noteworthy). These rules do not so much result in a prioritizing of the unity of God understood as prior to the persons, but rather shape the whole of Trinitarian theology. Gregory offers a fascinating example of how well a fourth century author could grasp the fundamental importance of such a move to the good practice of theology.

19　On this letter see, most recently, G. Christopher Stead, "Why not Three Gods?: The Logic of Gregory of Nyssa's Trinitarian Doctrine", in Hubertus R. Drobner and Christoph Klock (eds) *Studien zu Gregor von Nyssa und Die Christlichen Spätantike* (Leiden: E. J. Brill, 1990), pp. 149–163. Stead's article considers only the logic of differentiation (almost entirely what I have designated argument A). Stead notes that the argument is a logical one applicable to the differentiation of material things and angels, but then insists—on the weak grounds that Gregory argues his logical point from the example of three humans and usually about three biblical saints that (p. 160)—"underlying Gregory's confusion is the thought that ideal humanity, the human race at its best, would provide an analogy for the Holy Trinity". Unlike many modern commentators Stead thinks Gregory is deeply confused, and he refrains from endorsing his understanding of the project as a whole. Stead exemplifies the same problem as the earlier article by Turcescu considered in n. 7: he presents us with the evidence for concluding that Gregory does not intend to draw any detailed or dense analogy between three people and the triune God, but still insists that this is precisely Gregory's intention.

20   GNO III/1, 42; NPNF V, 332: "'Hear, O Israel, the Lord thy God is one Lord', even though the name of Godhead extends through the Holy Trinity. This I say according to the account we have given in the case of human nature, in which we have learnt that it is improper to extend the name of the nature by the mark of plurality. We must, however, more carefully examine the name of 'Godhead'."

21   *CE* III, 4 (GNO II/2, 36ff.; NPNF V, 146).

22   Gregory of Nyssa, *Apology on the Hexameron* (PG 44, 92). On this understudied text see Eugenio Corsini, "Nouvelles perspectives sur le probleme des sources de l'Hexaëméron de Grégoire de Nysse", *Studia Patristica*, II:I (1957), pp. 94–103; John F. Callahan, "Greek Philosophy and the Cappadocian Cosmology", *Dumbarton Oaks Papers* XII (1958), pp. 29–58.

23   For the moment Stead, "Why Not Three Gods?" remains the basis for future discussion.

24   *CE* II, 106 (GNO I/1, 256; NPNF V, 261).

25   GNO III/1, 43; NPNF V, 332.

26   E.g., Basil, *CE* I, 14–15; II, 32 (SC 299, 220ff.; SC 305, 132ff); Gregory of Nyssa, *C.E.* VII, 4–5 (GNO I/2, 178–184; NPNF V, 197–199).

27   A paradigmatic text in Gregory discussing this theme is *Contra Eunomium* II (GNO I/1, 256ff.; NPNF V, 260ff.). Here I have simply outlined some key aspects of Gregory's use in this context, the term itself has a long history even if we think only of Greek Christian writing. Foundational for Gregory's usage is Origen's in his *Comm. In Joh.* I.

28   Gregory of Nyssa, *CE* II (GNO I/1 270; NPNF V, 265).

29   See also *In Cant.* I (GNO VI, 36–38); trans. C. McCambley OCSO, Gregory of Nyssa, *Commentary on the Song of Songs* (Brookline MA: Hellenic College Press, 1987), pp. 53–54.

30   See Michel René Barnes, "Eunomius of Cyzicus and Gregory of Nyssa: Two traditions of Transcendental Causality", *Vigiliae Christianae* 52 (1998), pp. 59–87, here p. 81. See also Michel René Barnes *The Power of God: Dunamis in Gregory of Nyssa's Trinitarian Theology* (Washington, DC: Catholic University of America Press, 2000), pp. 297–305. Here Barnes notes that in *On Not Three Gods* Gregory makes significant use of *energeia* (energy) language to supplement his use of *dunamis*—the persons are one in *energeia* as well as *dunamis*. On the one hand, Barnes attributes this to the significance of *energeia* in debates over the Spirit: treating the Spirit as an *energeia* indicated to some a subordinate ontological status while, for pro-Nicenes an *energeia* was an expression of a *dunamis* and thus appeal to the same language could help to bolster a theology of the Spirit's full divinity. On the other hand, Barnes notes that this shift involves no fundamental change to Gregory's basic metaphysical or theological picture and thus I do no more than note it here.

31   Plotinus, *Ennead*, V.1.6.

32   Plotinus, *Ennead*, V.4.2.

33   See Michel René Barnes, "The Background and Use of Eunomius' Causal Language", in Michel Barnes and Daniel H. Williams (eds) *Arianism after Arius: Essays on the Development of the Fourth Century Trinitarian Conflicts* (Edinburgh: T. & T. Clark, 1993), pp. 217–236. Barnes's paper is concerned primarily with the presence of the sequence essence, activity, product in Eunomius and its precendents. However, *en passant* he remarks on the significance that stems from Gregory's retention of "power" in the sequence between essence and activity. This different sequence helps to shape a very different account of divine causality. In Eunomius's sequence and tradition the link between essence and activity is not a necessary one and thus, deploying such a sequence to describe the Son as "product" of the Father's activity serves to indicate the necessary subordination (and lack of co-eternity) that the Son must possess. Gregory, on the other hand, retains "power" in the sequence and, because a power is intrinsic to a nature and necessarily contains the causal capacity of that nature, speaking of the Son as the Father's power helps to shape a very different account of the divine generation.

34   GNO III/1, 44; NPNF V, 333. Cf. Origen, *Peri Archon* I, 2, 12, 411–416 (SC 252, 138) (cited by Barnes, "Background and Use", p. 231) for a direct precedent. Cf. *CE* I, 30–32 (GNO I/1, 152ff.; NPNF V, 75–76), where the same threefold sequence and the same virtual equivalence of power and nature is to be found.

35 GNO III/1, 44; NPNF V, 332–333: "Hence it is clear that by any of the terms we use the Divine Nature is not itself signified, but some one of its surroundings is made known ... Since, then, as we perceive the varied operations of the power above us, we fashion our appellations from the several operations that are known to us ... He surveys all things and overlooks them all, discerning our thoughts, and even entering by His power of contemplation those things that are not visible, [hence] we suppose that Godhead (*theotes*) is so called from beholding (*thea*) ... Now ... let him consider this operation, and judge whether it belongs to one of the persons whom we believe in the Holy Trinity, or whether the power extends throughout the Three Persons ... For Scripture attributes the act of seeing equally to Father, Son and Spirit." This text illustrates Gregory's deployment of the sequence nature-power-activity. Power and nature are, on the one hand, virtually synonymous and, on the other hand, it is the power that is the cause of actions *ad extra*.

36 It is frequently asserted that a fundamental "Cappadocian" theme is that natures are known by their operations. One of the purposes of the last few pages is to show that, in the specific case of Gregory of Nyssa, this account is not quite accurate. For Gregory operations reveal powers, natures remain unknown.

37 GNO III/1, 46; NPNF V, 333.

38 GNO III/1, 47; NPNF V, 334: "Thus, since among men the action of each in the same pursuits is discriminated, they are properly called many, since each of them is separated from the others within his own environment, according to the special character of his operation."

39 For the discussion in *Ad Graecos* see esp. GNO III/1, 23–24; trans. Daniel F. Stramara, Jr., *Greek Orthodox Theological Review* 41 (1996), pp. 381–391, here 384–385.

40 GNO III/1, 50; NPNF V, 334.

41 Unless we take the mere ascription of a distinct role and a distinct name within the divine action to indicate psychological content. If we do so, our language has become so general that we might just as well attribute "psychological" content to the discrete parts of the computer on which this paper is being written. However, just to repeat, my point is not that Gregory does not conceive of the persons as truly distinct, but that ascribing true distinctness to the Trinitarian persons is not necessarily equivalent to ascribing autonomous "personal" or "psychological" content to each of them.

42 This we have already seen in discussion of Gregory's *Hexameron*.

43 E.g., GNO III/1, 48; NPNF V, 334: "From Him, I say, who is the chief source of gifts, all things which have shared in this grace have obtained their life. When we inquire, then, whence this good gift came to us, we find, *by the guidance of the Scriptures* that it was from the Father, the Son and the Spirit." (italics added)

44 GNO III/1, 48; NPNF V, 334.

45 GNO III/1, 55; NPNF V, 336.

46 GNO III/1, 57; NPNF, V, 336 (italics added by NPNF translator).

47 Gregory of Nyssa, *Ref.*, 6 (GNO I/2, 328; NPNF V, 107).

48 Non Patristic specialists should note that the *CE* II which appears as NPNF V, 101ff. is actually *Refutation of Eunomius's Confession*; the true *CE* II appears as NPNF V, 250ff.

49 *In Cant.* I (GNO VI, 36–38; McCambley, 53–54).

50 Although I have hinted at most relevant themes for understanding the links between Gregory's account of divine power, ontological difference and the *askesis* of Christian thinking in this paper, a more extended discussion would need also to explore Gregory's account of how created powers (and the power of human life and thought) participate in the divine power—the Word—both now and through the process of salvation and sanctification.

51 Hanson, *The Search*, p. 730.

52 One unexplored theme in twentieth (and twenty-first) century appropriation of early Christian thought is the way in which the articulation of a theology of creation and of the distinction between Creator and creation is central to the articulation of the nature of salvation itself. Here one might compare the structure of Nyssa's thought with that of Augustine. For both it is the discourse of faith that begins to provide and begins to enable description of the order of things and God. The seduction of modern theologians into a post-Kantian and post-Barthian discussion whose parameters are "natural theology" or "revelation" have for sometime severely hampered engagement with the sorts of theological options seen in Nyssa or Augustine.

53 These themes may be particularly clearly seen in Gregory's homily on 1 Cor. 15:28 (PG 44, 1304–26). There is a detailed discussion of the text in Reinhard M. Hübner, *Die Einheit des Leibes Christi bei Gregor von Nyssa* (Leiden: E. J. Brill, 1974), pp. 27–66. Part of the significance of this text lies in the way that it shows particularly clearly how the polemical conflict around the Son's status and what I have termed the grammar of divinity had, for Gregory, clearly soteriological consequences. See also *CE* V, 5 where Gregory discusses the transformation of the Christian through the indwelling of God's power: this discussion nicely opens a number of avenues for investigating distinct technical backgrounds to the *theosis* theme that has so fascinated modern writers.

54 Karl Holl, *Amphilochius von Ikonium in seinem Verhältnis zu den grossen Kappadoziern* (Tübingen: J. C. B. Mohr, 1904), p. 209ff.

55 Most succinctly, Lienhard, "Ousia and hypostasis".

3

DIVINE UNITY AND THE DIVIDED SELF: GREGORY OF NYSSA'S TRINITARIAN THEOLOGY IN ITS PSYCHOLOGICAL CONTEXT

MICHEL RENÉ BARNES

Introduction

In the last hundred years Gregory of Nyssa's Trinitarian theology has received a substantial amount of attention. While those reading Gregory have come from a variety of denominational perspectives, in almost all cases Gregory's Trinitarian theology has been treated as a paradigm for a certain kind of Trinitarian theology. Indeed, today the most common understanding of the content and significance of Gregory's theology is that it is such a paradigm. In the same period of time Gregory's psychology has been studied extensively, primarily from the perspective of determining his philosophical sources and the degree or character of their influence upon his theology. Source questions have usually revolved around the two options of Platonic or Stoic.[1] Such source questions have had a mirrored presence in dogmatic histories. To a large extent these investigations were driven by a desire either to remove Gregory's credibility as a Christian theologian by impugning his theology as simply philosophical Hellenism (so from Liberal Christianity), or to defend Gregory from such attacks by revealing the fundamentally evangelical character of that theology (so from traditional Christianity).

The Trinitarian paradigm that Gregory represents has come more and more to be understood as centered upon *the Trinity as Three Persons*. At the same time, the notion of "person" has come more and more to be understood in the categories of "relation[ship]" or "consciousness".[2] The obvious effect

Michel René Barnes
Department of Theology, Marquette University, 100 Coughlin Hall, Milwaukee, WI 53201, USA

of such moves is that Gregory's Trinitarian theology is re-stated either as *The Trinity as "personal relationship"* or as *Locating consciousness(es) in the Trinity*. Often there is an assumption that when traditional thought is re-stated from a modern or contemporary perspective such re-statement renders the thought more complex and sophisticated—when, in fact, more often than not such re-statements simplify the original. In Gregory's case, what has been lost is an awareness of what he is himself most concerned with, or the context in which he is developing his theology. Strangely, despite the fact that Gregory's Trinitarian theology is appropriated because of its perceived psychological content, the scholarly studies of Gregory's psychology have not been sought out as resources for elaborating that psychology.[3] However (and this is important), while a knowledge of Gregory's psychology reveals its role in his Trinitarian theology, it also makes clear that *personal relationship* or *consciousness* are not the important, substantial psychological concepts for Gregory. Gregory's psychology takes its fundamental shape from a concern for the integrity of the will in its action, and, as a corollary, the character and redress of impediments to the action of the will.[4]

Most considerations of the psychological content of Gregory's Trinitarian theology begin with his Trinitarian theology and work to some kind of psychology. I will start from Gregory's psychology and work to his Trinitarian theology. In a general way this movement repeats Gregory's own, for he first writes his major treatises on psychology, and then next writes his major treatises on the Trinity. The major treatises on psychology from this time are *On the Soul and Resurrection* and *On the Making of Mankind* (one might also include his *Life of Macrina*, which is also written at this time); his major treatises on the Trinity from this time are the books against Eunomius; also included is the *Catechetical Oration*, which dates between 383 and 386. Two of the "short" Trinitarian treatises, *On the Trinity* and *On "Not Three Gods"* (the most elaborate), as well as *On the Holy Spirit*, are also written in the years from 380 to 383.[5] In short, I intend to look at what traditional psychological concerns are for Gregory, and to see how these concerns go along with his use of psychological language in a Trinitarian context.[6]

The Classical Phenomenology of the Will

Gregory's earliest writings are typically described as being "ascetic" in genre, but it would be just as accurate (and more helpful) to say that Gregory wrote moral psychology—or even, just "psychology." To speak of these writings as ones of "psychology" cues us instantly to the continuities between Gregory's psychology and other psychologies of the day.[7] Gregory's earliest writing, *On Virginity* (371?), is certainly an "ascetic" work, but the true subject of the piece is the repair of the soul[8] in which Gregory draws significantly from the moral psychologies of his time, especially the Stoic.[9] There were, it should be noted, hardly any purely descriptive works on psychology in Gregory's day: interest in the character or nature of the soul was consistently governed by moral concerns, and the analysis driven by these concerns was couched in competing accounts of the nature of the soul. Whether the focus is on the nature of the soul itself, or on the relationship of the soul to the body (e.g., the localization of functions or parts of the soul in parts of the body), the interest is still fundamentally moral.[10] Insofar as "consciousness" was a topic in classical—ancient and Hellenistic—psychology, it was predominantly as a moral phenomenon.[11]

As a moral phenomenon what was most striking and problematic about "consciousness" was its fractured character, the experience of a consciousness divided against itself.[12] Moral psychology began with the phenomenon of an internal conflict, not simply of "not *doing* the good that one willed" but of *feeling* what one did not want to feel. The most famous illustration of the problem of this internal conflict is the case of Leontius, which Plato repeats in *Republic* IV (440a) to deploy his own account of the soul. Briefly, while walking the walls of Athens, Leontius found himself attracted to the sight of the exposed bodies of those executed for instigating civil war. Leontius knows that such an attraction—indeed, such a pleasure—is wrong, but the desire is strong. The crisis is resolved by another "part" of Leontius arising within himself, virtually to "shout down" or at least to shame his immoral desire. This story is offered by Plato to support his positing of the conflicted moral state of humans; countless other examples, similarly motivated, could be provided as well from a wide variety of ancient and Hellenistic authors.[13]

The nature or identity of conflicting motivations could be expressed in a variety of ways, and the competition between these ways meant that any psychology was inevitably polemical in its form, since an author chose one approach rather than another.[14] For some, the rational constituted a separate soul from the irrational. At the other end of the spectrum (with a variety of opinions in between) was the opinion that such conflicting motivations were not in themselves outside the realm of reason, but that the overwhelming majority of people lacked the knowledge and discipline which could bring the feelings into proper order. Similarly, there was a variety in the understandings of what kind of existence the sources of these feelings had. Some related the different motivations or drives to different essences in the soul, each situated in a different part of the body, such that it was meaningful to speak of the different "parts" of the soul. Others spoke of a single soul or essence but with different faculties which corresponded to the different kinds of motivations. Finally, some thought that there was only one faculty, and that all motivations occurred in this one site. Even within a specific school there could be significant differences: Plotinus regarded the intellectual soul as in itself "undescended"—still "up" in the intelligible realm—while Iamblichus regarded the intellectual soul as "descended"—there was nothing left "up there".[15] One "catalogue" of moral psychologies from the time lists the basic options as follows: "Some think that man is made from a body and a triple soul; but others think that he is from a body and a soul having three powers; and again, some say that it is a question of a body, of a partial mind, of a soul and of the spirit which firms up this flabby body. Still others compose man ... of a twofold soul and a twofold mind."[16]

Gregory's Psychology: On the Soul and the Resurrection *and* On the Making of Mankind

The first of Gregory's own works on psychology is entitled *On the Soul and the Resurrection* (late 379 or 380?). Ever since Aristotle, treatises "on the soul" were standard for treating human psychology, especially for giving accounts of the structure or organization of the soul. Gregory's *On the Soul and the Resurrection* takes the form of a dialogue between himself and his elder sister, Macrina; the conversation is ostensibly the one that occurred between them the night before she died, events that Gregory describes in his *Life of Macrina*.[17] The dominant question of the majority of the dialogue is the status of emotions, their "structural" and their moral status. If emotions are judged to be morally problematic, then the structural question is whether emotions are an intrinsic or essential feature of our psychic makeup. Macrina's reflection on the issue is shaped by reflection on Gen. 1:25, which leads her to think of human nature in terms of being "the image and likeness of God", to ask whether emotions are part of human nature as originally created, and in general to frame her questions in causal and temporal categories (e.g., what is the cause of emotions, how does this cause relate to other psychic causes in us, and when did this cause become a part of our soul?). Macrina represents a psychology that externalized emotions, and the "drama" of the dialogue is furnished by Gregory finding such a psychology unsatisfactory.

The main aspects of the psychology of *On the Soul and the Resurrection* can be illustrated from a close reading of one passage.

> Upon this I [Gregory] returned to the definition which she had previously given of the soul, and I said that to my thinking it had not indicated distinctly enough all the powers of the soul, which are a matter of observation. Her definition declares the soul to be an intellectual essence [οὐσία], which imparts to the organic body the power [δύναμις] of life by which the senses operate [ἐνέργειαν]. Now the soul is not thus operative only in our scientific and speculative intellect; it does not produce results in that world only, or employ the organs of sense only for this their natural work. On the contrary, we observe in our nature many emotions of desire and many of anger; and both these exist in us as qualities of our kind, and we see both of them in their manifestations displaying further many most subtle differences. There are many states, for instance, which are occasioned by desire; many other states proceed from anger; and none of any of these are of the body; but that which is

not of the body is plainly intellectual. Now our definition exhibits the soul as something intellectual; so that one of two alternatives, both absurd, must emerge when we follow out this view to this end; either anger and desire are both second souls in us, and a plurality of souls must take the place of the single soul, or the thinking faculty in us cannot be regarded as a soul either (if they are not), the intellectual element adhering equally to all of them and stamping them all as souls, or else excluding every one of them equally from the specific qualities of soul.

You are quite justified, she [Macrina] replied, in raising this question, and it has before this been discussed by many elsewhere; namely, what we are to think of the principle of desire and the principle of anger within us. Are they coessential with the soul, inherent in the soul's very self from her first organization, or are they something different, accruing to us afterwards.[18]

We learn much from this passage. First, we are given a definition of soul, in which it is described as intellectual, meaning rational and immaterial, and yet the only functions of the soul specified are those relating to the material world (in this case, the body and the senses). Any problem of "How does an immaterial entity affect a material one?" is presumed away, removing potential difficulties not simply from the realm of psychology but also from theology (e.g., the rational, immaterial God acts upon the material world). Next, in this definition the soul is described as a cause: Gregory says that the soul imparts to the body the power of life, and we can imagine that any sort of Trinitarian theology which follows psychological modeling would have a precedent for thinking of the divine life in causal categories. Third, the causality of the soul is described in the technical language of οὐσία, δύναμις and ἐνέργεια. The psychological application of this aetiological analysis has its beginning in Aristotle's *On the Soul* and thereafter becomes a commonplace: see, e.g., works *On the Soul* by Tertullian and by Iamblichus (or the discussion of these by Festugière).[19] Fourth, Gregory here uses Platonic tripartite terminology to name the problematic psychological causes or parts, i.e., "desire" and "anger", ἐπιθυμετικόν and θυμός (the third is λογιστικόν). Fifth, desire and anger are each described specifically as a "cause" that produces multiple effects. Sixth, the existence of these causal sites poses the problem of whether there are "multiple souls" because: (a) How can anything of the sort of desire and anger be described as "rational" and thus belonging to a rational soul; and (b) How can anything which is one (e.g., the soul) produce effects which are different in kind? Seventh, the technical or scholastic character of Gregory's question is explicitly acknowledged in the dialogue by Macrina. Eighth, the eclectic or syncretistic nature of Gregory's psychology is made clear by the mix of terminologies (e.g., Platonic and Aristotelian). Finally, we see how it is that classical psychology is indeed developed in response to the experience of a consciousness divided against itself, that is, the experience of a divided will, and that the goal of any such psychology is to give an account of the soul which overcomes that experience of division (in Platonism, chiefly by identifying that psychic unit which is not divided against itself). This last point is different in kind from the previous eight, as it raises something like a hermeneutical question, namely, what are the inherent limitations in applying to a simple God terminology designed to identify and overcome a structure of psychic division?

For the moment we can summarize the psychological analysis in the selection from *On the Soul and the Resurrection* as follows: the will is ineffective in its attachment to the good; this lack of effectiveness is due to what is experienced as a conflict in the will; and this conflict suggests divisions in the will, i.e., the will is not meaningfully—as a moral agent—one with itself. For the future we expect that each of these three points in the analysis will figure in any psychological description of the Trinity.

The second treatise by Gregory on human psychology and anthropology is *On the Making of Mankind*, probably written shortly after *On the Soul and the Resurrection*, just as Gregory was beginning the first book of his *Against Eunomius* (*Contra Eunomium*) in 380.[20] It is regularly remarked by scholars that the work is a kind of *Hexameron* piece, in that it is styled as an exegesis of "six days" material in Genesis; in this case the focus is on Gen. 1:25 (a text already important in *On the Soul and the Resurrection*). Included in *On the Making of Mankind* is a substantial treatment of the physiological constitution of humans, and in general the work is more concerned with the interaction of mind and body than is *On the Soul and the Resurrection*.[21] The two works can usefully be regarded as complementary accounts of human nature, which, in their two areas of focus reflect the classical ways of framing an account of what is specific to human nature.[22]

While *On the Soul and the Resurrection* shows no awareness of the Trinitarian controversies raging around its author, *On the Making of Mankind* begins with an argument against the anti-Nicene Trinitarian theology of Eunomius and his followers. Gregory's argument for the unity of God is significant for our purposes.

And let no one suppose me to say that the Deity is in touch with existing things in a manner resembling human *operation*, by means of different *powers*. For it is impossible to conceive in the simplicity of the Godhead the varied and diverse nature of the apprehensive *operation*: not even in our own case are the faculties which apprehend things numerous, although we are in touch with those things which affect our life in many ways by means of our senses; for there is one *power*, the implanted mind itself, which passes through each of the organs of sense and grasps the things beyond....

If in men, then, even though the organs formed by nature for purposes of perception may be different, that which operates and moves by means of all, and uses each appropriately for the object before it, is one and the same, not changing its nature by the differences of *operations*, how could any one suspect multiplicity of *essence* in God on the ground of His varied *powers*?[23]

In short, *If the mind does many different things, but still remains one, then we can reason that God's unity is not fractured by his diverse operations.* The terminology for the different elements of this analysis is key: there is mind, νοῦς, which is described as a power or faculty, δύναμις; this faculty produces and monitors many different operations, ἐνεργείαι. Neither the case of a multiplicity of powers nor that of a multiplicity of operations is evidence of fundamental divisions—i.e., different essences—in the existent that acts, whether mind or God.

Two different polemics come together in this passage. The first is the traditional debate in classical psychology over whether different psychological faculties must be understood as existing in different essences or souls (or parts of the body). Platonists tend to say yes; Gregory comes down more on the side of the Aristotelians, who say no. The second polemical context is the engagement with the anti-Nicene theology of Eunomius. One peculiarity of Eunomius' Trinitarian theology is his argument that since each different operation comes from a separate cause (which Eunomius calls οὐσία, not δύναμις),[24] the different operations of producing the Son and producing the Spirit are the effects of different essences: the Father and the Son are thus different in essence.[25] Such fine distinctions in aetiologies are of central importance to the Trinitarian theologies of the Eunomian controversy and especially of Gregory of Nyssa.[26] In Gregory's writings of substance against Eunomius he will argue that since the Father, Son, and Holy Spirit can be shown to possess the same power, they must then have the same nature. This argument turns upon the philosophically developed understanding that certain capabilities (δύναμις) are exclusive to specific natures, as burning is to fire.[27] In *On the Making of Mankind*, however, Gregory is offering a psychological analogy to the Trinity, the first of a number of analogies—psychological and otherwise—he will utilize in his writings.[28]

Given that the subject of this essay is how traditional psychological concerns go along with Gregory's use of psychological language in a Trinitarian context, there is one other significant argument in *Making of Mankind* which needs to be noted, one which again draws upon the resemblance between the human mind and God. Again working from Gen. 1:25, Gregory says that the origin of our free will lies in our resemblance to the divine.

The language of Scripture therefore expresses it concisely by a comprehensive phrase, in saying that man was made "in the image of God": for this is the same as to say that He made human nature participant in all good; for if the Deity is the fullness of good, and this is His image, then the image finds its resemblance to the Archetype in being filled with all good.

Thus there is in us the principle of all excellence, all virtue and wisdom, and every higher thing that we conceive: but pre-eminent among
all is the fact that we are free from necessity, and not in bondage to any
natural power, but have decision in our own power as we please; for
virtue is a voluntary thing, subject to no dominion: that which is the
result of compulsion and force cannot be virtue.[29]

This needs to be noted. In Gregory's psychology, the attribution of a capacity
to will is not derived from existence as individual(s), or from the existence
of individuals in "relation": the cause of its existence is wholly unrelated to
the reality of individual existence. The existence of a will in an existent is
determined by its nature; the *kind* of will an existent possesses is determined
by its specific nature. Animals, for example, have different kinds of wills
than we humans do.[30] God has a *free* will because a free will is one
of the perfections of the divine nature. Free will follows from the kind of
nature, namely, the perfect nature of divinity: the Perfect Life wills perfectly,
i.e., it wills freely.[31] In short, simply to attribute a will to each of the Three
establishes nothing about their common nature, for it presumes the answer
to the very question at issue, *What is the nature of each of the Three*? We must
know what kind of nature the Son and Holy Spirit each have so we can know
what kind of will they have (and vice versa).[32]

The Significance of Ὑπόστασις

Some time ago J. H. Srawley remarked—apropos of Gregory's *Catechetical
Oration* (or the *Great Catechism*)—that the term ὑπόστασις "denotes 'a particular center of being'" and has a different meaning than "person."[33] Similar
judgments have been offered since then with some regularity, and yet the
habit of translating and treating ὑπόστασις as "person" has continued
unabated.[34] Sometimes even those scholars who demonstrate for us that
Gregory does not use ὑπόστασις as a psychological term, but rather as,
e.g., a term of predication, themselves continue to treat ὑπόστασις as though
Gregory meant something in the realm of psychological discourse. We must
be very clear: Gregory uses ὑπόστασις to mean an existent with real and
separate existence, and he does not use the term to refer to or to name a subject of cognition or volition.

Ὑπόστασις especially has the sense of "individual" when it is set in
relation to the categories or language of either οὐσία or φύσις. The formula
of distinction—"one οὐσία/φύσις, three ὑποστάσεις"—specifies the language pairing in which the terms are to be understood, as if to say: "When
οὐσία and ὑπόστασις are used together to describe the Trinity, we must
necessarily say one οὐσία and three ὑποστάσεις." Implied here is that when
ὑπόστασις is not used with οὐσία or φύσις, the same rule might not apply.[35]
The reasons for setting the oppositional field to "οὐσία-ὑπόστασις" were

primarily historical, not logical.[36] By historical, not logical I mean that bishops in the fourth century did not come to formulate the linked definition of the specific terms οὐσία and ὑπόστασις because ὑπόστασις was the uniquely clear and distinct term to use, but because the term was already in play in the Christian tradition.[37]

What we can say about Gregory's understanding of ὑπόστασις is that it is intimately tied to the broader shape of his Trinitarian theology and, it should be noted, to what is new in that theology. In particular, unlike the theology of Nicaea, 325, and that of Athanasius, Cappadocian theology does not use "generation" to ground a doctrine of "common nature" or "one essence" in the Trinity. Where Athanasius and his contemporaries use the doctrine of divine generation to prove that the Father and Son have the same nature or essence, Gregory uses generation as the basis for distinguishing the Persons. This is a major development, and it is only within the context of this new move that can one understand how and why Gregory uses ὑπόστασις as he does.

In the late 350s those who supported the council and creed of Nicaea, 325, argued that the language of Father and Son referred to a relationship in which the offspring has the same nature as the source. A parent's child is always the same nature as the parent. In the case of the Trinity, if the Father was indeed a father and the Son was indeed a son, then the kind of generation by the Father which produced the Son was that kind in which a nature was communicated from source to offspring. Being from the Father's essence, the Son was of the same essence. In the 350s, then, the theological "work" of Father-Son language was to ground the continuity of essence between the Two.[38] This in itself marks a development from the original theology of Nicaea, 325, in which the burden of the argument for continuity of nature is carried directly by essence language, and a reader of the creed could be left wondering (as some were) if "Father" and "Son" referred simply to the Incarnation. Such a limitation on what the two titles referred to was not intended—as it would be today—to negate doctrinal assertions about pre-Incarnation; rather, in the "logic" of the theology of Nicaea, 325, statements about the divinity of the Son were being made through the concepts and language of οὐσία, and not through "Father–Son" language.[39] What "Father–Son" language was *not* doing was grounding any doctrine of the separate existences of the Two.[40]

It is not too much of a cliché to say that in the second half of the fourth century there are thus two arguments to be made among those favoring Nicaea: how to argue for the single or common nature in the Trinity, and how to argue for the separate reality of each of the Three (even if polemically most of the attention is focused on the Two).[41] Gregory's arguments for both of these points marks off a new stage in Nicene theology, and, as I said above, the sense Gregory gives to ὑπόστασις is very much a part of this new stage.

In Gregory's Trinitarian theology, the generation of the Son by the Father is the basis of his doctrine of the reality of the distinct existences of those

Two. The Father–Son relationship is not the basis for his arguing for a common nature or essence between the Two.[42] At times Gregory seems to pare that relationship down to its simplest terms—namely, Cause and Caused—and he has taken some criticism from moderns for this move. I think that such criticism comes out of the expectation that psychological entities ("persons") really are fundamental to Gregory's exposition of the Trinity, when they are not, and in this way modern problems with Gregory's causal language are related to the equally modern idea that ὑπόστασις means "person". One of the most direct statements by Gregory of his argument for the real existence and identities of the Three occurs at the end of *On "Not Three Gods"*, and this passage can usefully be quoted here:

> while we confess the invariable character of the nature,[43] we do not deny the difference in respect of cause, and that which is caused, *by which alone we apprehend that one [person][44] is distinguished from another*; by our belief, that is, that one is the Cause, and another is of the Cause…. since the idea of cause differentiates the Persons of the Holy Trinity, declaring that one exists without a Cause, and another is of the Cause….[45]

By this succinct argument Gregory articulates his doctrine of the reality of the individuality of the Three. The argument is particularly interesting because it both receives and transforms previous Nicene theology: on the one hand, the traditional concerns for the uncaused character of the Father are clearly represented, but, on the other hand, the unqualified use of "uncaused" no longer functions as the criterion of divinity.[46] The relationship of the Son to the Father is still of central importance, but for a different reason than it was before. Where before in Nicene theology the reality of the titles "Father" and "Son" guaranteed that there was a natural relationship (a continuity of nature or unity of essence) between these Two, now that reality guarantees that there is some difference in existence between the Two so entitled.[47] The character of that difference is expressed in terms of causality; the reality of that difference is expressed by the term ὑπόστασις.

Given the context for Gregory's concern over unity and individuality in the Trinity, it is hard to see how asserting the psychological character of the Three or the social reality of the One would advance any argument against his opponents. How does arguing that the Three are each psychological entities make the reality of their individuality more certain? How, exactly, would a Nicene Trinitarian theology be advanced by the assertion that there are in God multiple wills? Such an assertion is useful only to the degree that there is a prior understanding that a psychological entity ("person") is irreducible: "person" is then the intermediate concept by which one can assert the irreducibility of each of the Three.

Gregory had some reason to speak clearly about the reality of the separate existences of the Son and Holy Spirit. There were, in his time, two Trinitarian theologies that denied the individual reality of either of these Two. First, there was Marcellus of Ancyra, who was known for denying the real separate existence of the Word; his more radical protégé, Photinus, developed his theology further to a doctrine of the Word and Spirit as projections of the Father.[48] However, the more serious threat faced by Gregory was the anti-Nicene Trinitarian theology of Eunomius of Cyzicus. While no one could accuse Eunomius of impugning the reality of the Son,[49] the same was not true of his theology of the Spirit, whom he described as the "activity" of the Son. (The Son, by contrast, was an "essence" in his own right.) The Holy Spirit was the Son in action; the Spirit's "reality" was the Son. If the confrontation with Eunomian theology over the nature of the Son required Gregory to develop his argument for the Father and the Son having the "same nature", then equally Gregory's confrontation with Eunomian theology over the reality of the Holy Spirit required him to develop his argument for the Spirit's individual existence. The same is true for Gregory of Nazianzus, who says in 380:

> Now if He [the Holy Spirit] were an accident, He would be an activity of God, for what else, or of whom else, could He be, for surely this is what most avoids composition? And if He is an activity, He will be effected, but will not effect and will cease to exist as soon as He has been effected, for this is the nature of an activity. How is it then that He acts and says such and such things, and defines, and is grieved, and is angered, and has all the qualities which belong clearly to one that moves, and not to movement?[50]

This passage from Nazianzus is important for its description of Eunomian "minimalist" pneumatology, and, as well, for the way it clearly illustrates that what is at stake is not simply the "separate reality" of the Holy Spirit, but the Spirit's status as what we would call a "person": the Holy Spirit "acts and says such and such things, and defines, and is grieved, and is angered...." One other point should not be lost from reading the passage: Nazianzus stumbles in his ability to say what the Holy Spirit *is*, to say what kind of existence the Spirit has (i.e., "personal").[51] Gregory of Nyssa's writings on the Holy Spirit come after this *Oration* by Gregory of Nazianzus, and there is reason to believe that he understood the need for stronger and clearer language on both the distinct and the personal reality of the Holy Spirit— language which made clear that the Spirit *like the Son* was a psychological entity with a distinct existence. The circumstances of the era result in the fact that Gregory of Nyssa's most significant descriptions of the psychological character or nature of both the Son and the Holy Spirit occur only after the "Nicene" debate has become truly Trinitarian, that is, only after the question of status of the Spirit is substantially engaged. One work by Gregory that particularly reflects this is his *Catechetical Oration* (or *Great Catechism*).

Gregory's Psychology of the Trinity: *The Catechetical Oration*

Gregory several times offers descriptions of the real existence of the Son and Spirit; the language is largely technical, and the terminology largely overlaps from statement to restatement in the work. Gregory's description of the Son and Spirit in the *Catechetical Oration* brings together assertions grounding the reality of an individual existent with assertions grounding the psychological nature of that existent. I give both occasions of Gregory's definition—the one he gives of the Son and the one he gives of the Spirit—but I will focus on the second expression.

> [The Word is] … a self-subsisting existent [οὐσιωδῶς ὑφεστῶτα], with a faculty of moral choice [προαιρετικόν] ever-working, all-powerful.[52]

> [W]e conceive of the Spirit as an existent Power [δύναμις οὐσιῴδη], with its own existence [ἰδιαζούσῃ ὑποστάσει] … an individual [ὑπόστασιν οὖσαν], with a faculty of moral choice [προαιρετικήν], self-moved, active, always choosing what is good, and for its every purpose having a power [δύναμις] sufficient to its will [βουλή].[53]

First it will be useful to remember that earlier when Gregory argues in *Against Eunomius*, book I, that Eunomius is actually proposing a fourth member of the Trinity, namely, the energy (called "Father") that produces the Son, he says that Eunomius is making the energy "an existent Power, self-existing, bringing about expression by a voluntary motion".[54] Leaving aside the last qualification, Gregory here offers a basic definition of what he understands each of the Three to be. In the *Catechetical Oration*,[55] Gregory continues to use the same language, but the "psychological" description of the Individuals is further developed. What seems to be consistent throughout all of Gregory's definitions of the kind of existence each of the Three possesses is that Gregory first lays out the reality of the individual existence,[56] and next lays out the psychological content (if any) of that existence.[57] The two descriptions are connected, but they are not identical, and, most importantly, there is no overarching concept or term which names them both or together: there is thus no concept of "person" as we tend to mean it.

A few words glossing the definition might be helpful. The phrase "existent Power" is Gregory's term for fully existent or real ("transcendentally real"). The ancient basis for Gregory's language here is Plato's *Sophist* 247D, where "the mark of the real" is that it possesses the power to affect,[58] and Gregory certainly understands "real" to include the power to affect. While hypostatic language figures significantly in Gregory's assertion of the reality of individual existence, the sense of the terminology remains simply that of "individual existence".[59] That the existent in question is one with the ability to make moral choices is announced by Gregory's choice of terminology for that will, namely προαίρεσις (*prohairesis*) or some derivative. The term is Aristotelian in origin, but was developed into a more significant term in moral psychology by Epictetus, for whom (and thereafter) it has virtually the sense of "moral personality".[60] By contrast, Gregory's language of "self-moved, active" is about as generic a description of something that is alive as is possible: the original and more typical provenance of the two terms is as descriptions of soul. Finally, we come to Gregory's description of the moral perfection of such an Individual: the will does not fail to decide for the good, and having decided, the will has the integrity and strength to will the good it has decided for. In its own way, positing the existence of such an effective, integral will is every bit a statement of divine otherness, God's transcendence, as the attribution of "existent Power" or full and perfect existence.

The Efficacy of God's Will

In this final section I will show that while Gregory may indeed be said to have a psychology of the Individuals of the Trinity, in the end that psychology maps out a radical difference between our self-experience and the "self-experience" of those Individuals. At the end of my treatment of *On the Soul and the Resurrection* I remarked that the ineffective moral character of the will would figure in any psychological description by Gregory of the Trinity.[61] It goes almost without saying that this ineffective character of the will is not something that Gregory would attribute to God, but rather something which is overcome in God. And indeed Gregory is emphatic, in his description of the wills of the Son and the Spirit, that they perfectly will the good and accomplish the good that they will. We must know, Gregory says, that the Word's will is completely effective, and

> that such a will has also capacity to act must be the conclusion of a devout mind. For if you admit not this potency, you prove the reverse to exist. But no; impotence is quite removed from our conception of Deity. Nothing of incongruity is to be observed in connection with the Divine nature, but it is absolutely necessary to admit that the power of that word is as great as the purpose, lest mixture, or concurrence, of contradictions be found in an existence that is incomposite, as would be the case if, in the same purpose, we were to detect both impotence and power, if, that is, there were power to do one thing, but no power to do something else.[62]

This part of Gregory's description of the psychological integrity of the Word has to do with His creative capacity: this is a question of cosmology and creation, and this is the traditional context for a statement about God's ability to act effectively. With Origen, for example, the question of the efficacy of God's will pertains to generation and creation (insofar as there is a difference for Origen), and is set within the context of questions of providence and dualism. Does God need anything else in order to create? Is there a co-eternal material substratum? The sufficiency of God's will for production becomes, for Origen, the basis for describing the Son as being generated by that very will. God did not intend to generate the Son, and then did generate, using other means (even if those means were never external to Him); the intention itself brings the Son into existence.[63]

The old context of providence (and what is by now a full doctrine of creation *ex nihilo*) still remains in Gregory's thought, for the act of creation continues to be a key subject of theological reflection and figures significantly in doctrines of the Trinity.[64] But the doctrine of divine sufficiency in creating is not the point here: the point is that the divine will is equal to the good, or more specifically, being equal to the good is one sign of a will being divine.[65] Thus the passage from *Catechetical Oration* that I began quoting just above continues in this way:

> Also we must suppose that this will in its power to do all things will have no tendency to anything that is evil (for impulse towards evil is foreign to the Divine nature), but that whatever is good, this it also wishes, and, wishing, is able to perform, and, being able, will not fail to perform; but that it will bring all its proposals for good to effectual accomplishment.

This emphasis on the ability of the Word and the Spirit successfully to will and do the good becomes, in the rest of the *Catechetical Oration*, the single measure of the potency and efficacy of their divine wills; creative potency is no longer referred to.[66] The integrity of the wills of the Son and Spirit are conspicuous and significant evidence that the Two are divine. If we wonder if, as with us, *the Son's will is ineffective in its attachment to the good*, we read from Gregory that "the Word ... works out effectually whatever He wills". If we wonder if *the Son experiences a conflict in the will*, we read that the Word "works out effectually whatever He wills by having a power concurrent with His will". If we wonder if *the Son's will is not one with itself*, we read that He is "very Power with an impulse to all good".[67] The reality of the Son's and Spirit's morally effective will—and the significance of that reality—is brought home all the more when we note that Gregory's most extensive statements to this effect[68] occurs not in the section of the *Catechetical Oration* devoted to the doctrine of the Trinity, but in the section which deals with the relative moral (im)perfection of human wills, where evil is described as originating from the failure of our wills. This brings us to something fundamental.

The integrity and effectiveness of the wills of the Son and Spirit stands in direct contrast to the state of our human wills. Our will is not one, or rather, we do not have only one will: we have many, and the conflict among them sabotages our own decisions. Not only can we not successfully will and do the good, we cannot even will what we have decided to will—what we "want" to will, as it were. However, in other ways Gregory's theology mitigates the otherness of a will that is one with itself by his judgment that some humans have attained an undivided, unconflicted will. Moses is such a one, according to Gregory in *On the Soul and Resurrection*,[69] and Macrina is portrayed as such a person in the *Life of Macrina*.[70] As some come more and more to resemble God, θεῶσις, their wills become more unified, and their co-willing with the Trinity more extended. In any case, while there may be a handful of people in the history of the human race who have attained to an undivided, unconflicted will, for the vast majority of us such a psychological state is unknown and unexperienced:[71] it is not our experience of our own will.[72] Moreover, even if it is the case that Gregory's ascetic doctrine of the Christian sage allows the possibility that a human will can be one with itself and that a few at least can indeed experience the reflected state of psychological integrity that we were originally created with, the psychology of the Trinity contains one other level of psychological unity to which humans cannot attain: the Individuals of the Trinity have wills which are not only one with themselves but perfectly one with the will of the other Two.[73] Perfect unity among wills, like unity within a will ("freedom"), is true only of wills with a divine nature—if this were otherwise then Gregory's argument that *unity of operations proves unity of nature* would have no standing. This Trinitarian argument depends upon the fundamentals articulated in *On the Making of Humanity*, namely, that the existence and kind of will anyone has is determined by the kind of nature that that one has.[74]

> For the *community of nature* [φύσεως κοινωνία] gives us warrant that the will of the Father, of the Son, and of the Holy Spirit is one, and thus, if the Holy Spirit wills that which seems good to the Son, the community of will [ἡ κοινωνία τοῦ θελήματος] clearly points to *unity of essence* [τῆς οὐσίας ἑνότητα].[75]

Each of the Three may be said to possess an integrated will, and the faculty which enacts that will, but we must be careful not to impose the implications of a later concept of "person" (e.g., Boethian or Cartesian) upon Gregory and make an erroneous presupposition. There is nothing in Gregory's writings which requires that the wills of each of the Three be conceived of as separate wills.[76] In a conceptual idiom where the existence of a faculty of cognitive volition collapses into the existence of real individuality—or vice versa—we can expect that each will exists uniquely and exclusively in a given individual. But this is not Gregory's conceptual idiom. Gregory may link cognitive volition to real individuality, but the two kinds of existences have different origins, and there is nothing to require that the two kinds of existences necessarily overlap ontologically. The limits of cognitive volition need not be the same as the limits of real individuality. In short, Three Individuals, but One Will throughout the Three, or, as Gregory puts it, "the motion of the divine will from the Father, through the Son, to the Spirit".[77] Gregory of

Nazianzus is perhaps even clearer on this point when he comments on the Scripture passage, "The Son came down from Heaven, not to do His own Will, but the Will of Him That sent Him":

> But since, as this [Scripture passage] is the language of Him Who assumed our Nature (for He it was Who came down), and not of the Nature which He assumed, we must meet the objection in this way, that the passage does not mean that the Son has a special will of His own, besides that of the Father, but that He has not; so that the meaning would be, "not to do Mine own Will, for there is none of Mine apart from, but that which is common to, Me and Thee; for as We have one Godhead, so We have one Will".[78]

Conclusion

Most modern readings of personhood and the Trinity in Gregory serve to circumscribe the sorts of discussions in which Gregory is taken to engage. Gregory is taken to say something that can be easily assimilated into the range of options available in modern discussions of the role of psychological language in Trinitarian theology. In postmodern terms one might say that the otherness of his language is domesticated by being read as easily assimilated to the contours of modern psychological and Trinitarian discourse. My argument here has shown that in order to become good readers of Gregory not only do we need to notice that he frequently does not advocate the positions modern have taken him to advocate, but, equally importantly, we need to understand that the contours of the discussions within which he is historically situated are very different from those of modern Trinitarian theologians. His true contribution to the discussion of psychology and Trinitarian theology may thus be to offer a reorientation of what should be discussed. Reading Gregory does not so much offer us opinions corresponding to an existing range of modern options, as it suggests that the very shape of what it means to use psychological terms in Trinitarian theology is different from modern expectations.[79]

NOTES

1   The foundational works on Gregory's sources were (chronologically): Karl Gronau, *Poseidonios und die Judisch-Christliche Genesisexegese* (Berlin: Ruck und Verlag von B. G. Teubner, 1914); Harold Cherniss, *The Platonism of Gregory of Nyssa* (1930; rpt., Berkeley: B. Franklin, 1970); Jean Daniélou, *Platonisme et théologie mystique; essai sur la doctrine spirituelle de Saint Grégoire de Nysse* (Paris: Aubier, Éditions Montaigne, 1944); John Cavarnos, "The Psychology of Gregory of Nyssa", Ph.D dissertation Harvard University, 1947, later substantially published as "The Relation of Body and Soul in the Thought of Gregory of Nyssa", in *Gregor von Nyssa und die Philosophie*, Heinrich Dörrie, ed (Leiden: E. J. Brill, 1976), pp. 61–78. These works are important as documents of a very influential effort to identify Gregory's philosophical sources, but as descriptions of the content of sources, or of Gregory's utilization of sources, they are obsolete.

2   By "relationship" I mean something of the order of "I-Thou" conceptualizing.

3   Recent significant works on Gregory's psychology include (chronologically): Gerhart B. Ladner, "The Philosophical Anthropology of Saint Gregory of Nyssa", *Dumbarton Oaks Papers*, XII (1958), pp. 61–94; Ton H. C. Van Eijk, "Marriage and Virginity, Death and Immortality", in *Epektasis*, Jacques Fontaine and Charles Kannengiesser, eds (Paris: Beauchesne, 1974), pp. 209–235; Catharine P. Roth, "Platonic and Pauline Elements in the Ascent of the Soul in Gregory of Nyssa's *Dialogue on the Soul and Resurrection*", *Vigiliae Christianae* 46 (1992), pp. 20–30; Rowan Williams, "Macrina's Deathbed: Gregory of Nyssa on Mind and Passion", in Lionel Wickham and Caroline Bammel, eds *Christian Faith and Greek Philosophy in Late Antiquity* (Leiden: E. J. Brill, 1993), pp. 227–246; and Michel René Barnes, "The Polemical Context and Content of Gregory of Nyssa's Psychology", *Journal of Medieval Philosophy and Theology* 4 (1994), pp. 1–24.

4   By "psychology" or "psychological" I mean *having to do with cognitive volition.*

5   Two early "short" treatises on the Trinity—*Ad Graecos* and *Ep.* 38—are written at the same time (379–380) as Gregory is writing *On the Soul and Resurrection* and *On the Making of Mankind.* Strangely, the two Trinitarian treatises, filled as they are with the language of πρόσωπον and ὑπόστασις (respectively), show no signs of the unequivocally psychological concerns Gregory is working through in the other writings. *On the Soul and Resurrection* shows no sensitivity to trinitarian concerns, while *On the Making of Mankind* engages with such concerns explicitly, and one can observe in *On the Making of Mankind* Gregory's explicit turn to trinitarian polemics while he is engaged primarily with writing a work on human psychology or anthropology. See my article, "The Polemical Context and Content of Gregory of Nyssa's Psychology", pp. 4 and 11.

6   *Life of Moses* and the *Commentary on the* Song of Songs are usually judged to be late works, dating from the late 380s or early 390s, shortly before Gregory died in 394 (5?).

7   A substantial introduction to Hellenistic psychology may be found in Julia Annas, *Hellenistic Philosophy of Mind* (Berkeley, CA: University of California Press, 1992). The standard study of Hellenistic psychology is Brad Inwood, *Ethics and Human Action in Early Stoicism* (Oxford: Clarendon Press, 1985). A useful collection of articles treating different classical psychologies is *Psychology*, Stephen Everson, ed, Companions to Ancient Thought, vol. 2 (Cambridge: Cambridge University Press, 1991). Two other works, different in subject and scope, are helpful to know: Henry J. Blumenthal, *Plotinus' Psychology: His Doctrines of the Embodied Soul* (The Hague: Martinus Nijhoff, 1971); and P. A. Vander Waerdt, "The Peripatetic Interpretation of Plato's Tripartite Psychology", *Greek Roman Byzantine Studies*, XXVI (1985), pp. 283–302.

8   "… while it [virginity] is the channel which draws down the Deity to share man's estate [i.e., in the virginal Incarnation], it keeps wings for man's desires to rise to heavenly things, and is a bond of union between the Divine and human, by its mediation bringing into harmony these existences so widely divided." *On Virginity* II, Nicene and Post Nicene Fathers, Second Series, V:345. Hereafter this series is abbreviated as NPNF.

9   See my "'The Burden of Marriage' and Other Notes on Gregory of Nyssa's *On Virginity*", *Studia Patristica* vol. 37, M. F. Wiles and E. J. Yarnold, eds (Leuven: Peters, 2001), pp. 12–19.

10 The physiological way of talking about the soul—locating certain parts or functions in specific organs—is supported by none other than Plato: one of the great ironies is that while he may have intended to replace a physical or material account of the soul with an immaterial description, his psychology was instead understood as overlaying an immaterial description upon a material.

11 It is important to remember that in classical psychology generally, "consciousness" was understood primarily as "willing" or "the will in action". To be conscious was to will, one experienced the fact of selfhood in the act of willing (not, as would later be the case, in an awareness of the fact that *I am willing*), and to have a divided consciousness was to have a divided will (or to have conflicting wills). (The best illustration of this classical understanding is, of course, Augustine's *Confessions*.) By and large, there was no static or steady-state understanding of the will: instead, the will is variously described as ever-moving, restless, or directed to(wards). This state of activity reflects the state of the soul itself, for the soul *acts*; indeed, as we shall see, the fact of this activity provides the substance of Gregory's premier definition of the soul.

12 This experience of a fractured consciousness and the tentativeness of the unified self is, I assume, a significant point of contact between pre-modern and post-modern sensibilities.

13 I am not here interested in the names or numbers of conflicting drives Plato identifies, but simply the fact that, for Plato, the basic story of the internal moral life of humans is one of conflict needing to be resolved.

14 The best (and most influential) illustration of the "polemical" character of Hellenistic psychology is provided by Galen, especially in his *On the Doctrines of Hippocrates and Plato*, three tomes, Phillip de Lacy, ed, trans., and comm., *Corpus Medicorum Graecorum*, vols 4.1,2 (Berlin: Akademie-Verlag, 1978, 1980, 1984).

15 It is important to be clear that not even for Plato was this "fracturedness" simply a matter of a mind-body opposition.

16 The catalogue is from Marius Victorinus, *Against Arius* 1A, in *Theological Treatises on the Trinity*, Mary Clark, trans. intro., and comm., Fathers of the Church vol. 69 (Washington, DC: Catholic University of America Press, 1981), p. 190. The very Neoplatonic Victorius claims the last psychology for his own understanding; a two-soul (rational, irrational) psychology is also articulated by (the seemingly unschooled) Macrina in *On the Soul and the Resurrection*.

17 Scholars have noted the resemblance in genre between Gregory's *On the Soul and the Resurrection* and Plato's dialogue, the *Phaedo*, which also gives an account of the soul, led by Socrates who is about to die. In this case, the dialogue form gives emphasis to the moral perspective on the matter at hand. Treatises "on the resurrection" are more specifically Christian in origin, and by Gregory's time are traditional works of apologetic. Christians began to write treatises on the resurrection as soon as they turned to the task of apology, in order to justify a doctrine which was especially perceived as bizarre and irrational by the surrounding Pagan culture.

18 The translation is from NPNF V:439, with some modification; for example, the NPNF translate σύνουσιωμένα with "consubstantial", which is, I think, misleading: I give "coessential". The Greek is from PG XLVI 48C–49B; there is, as yet, no critical edition of this work.

19 A. J. Festugière, *La révélation d'Hermès Trismégiste*, 4 vols (Paris: Société d'Éditions des Belles Lettres, 1949–1954).

20 See the very useful article by Eugenio Corsini, "La polemica contro Eunomio e la formazione della dottrina sulla creazione in Gregorio di Nisa", *Arché è Telos: L'anthropologia di Origene e di Gregorio di Nissa*, U. Bianci and H. Crouzel, eds (Milano: Universita Cattolica del Sacro Curore, 1981), pp. 197–216.

21 Gregory's *On the Making of Mankind* should be compared to Philo's work of the same name, as well as to the work by the Cappadocian protégé, Nemesius of Emesa, *On the Nature of Mankind*.

22 It is interesting to note that while modern constructions might expect Gregory to discover the most fundamental dualism in a "mind–body" tension, in fact the separation is experienced, according to Gregory, in the will.

23 *On the Making of Mankind* VI.1–2, NPNF V:391–392, emphasis added. In all cases, including plurals, "essence" is "οὐσία"; "power" is "δύναμις"; and "operation" is "ἐνέργεια".

24 Some scholarship has steadfastly maintained that an "essence–energy" distinction is introduced into late fourth century Greek theology by Basil of Caesarea. This understanding is wrong, since the distinction is used by Eunomius well in advance of Basil. See my "Background and Use of Eunomius' Causal Hierarchy", in *Arianism After Arius: Essays on the Development of the Fourth Century Trinitarian Conflicts*, M. Barnes and D. Williams, eds (Edinburgh: T. & T. Clark, 1993), pp. 217–236.

25 Eunomius' opinion that each different operation comes from a separate cause really is peculiar in the era. The much more typical judgment can be found in Origen's observation that, "By the one heat wax is melted and mud is dried". *On First Principles* III.I.11. Note from my opening descriptions of *On the Soul and the Resurrection* and *On the Making of Mankind* that both works invoke the psychological version of "single cause—multiple effects".

26 For a number of theologians and scholars, if one can make a case that Gregory's language for the Three is "relational" then one has shown that Gregory is asserting some kind of psychological or social existence for the Three. If ὑπόστασις or πρόσωπον is "relational", then it denotes a psychological or social relationship. Such a conclusion ignores the fact that there are many types of "relation", and, moreover, that there is clear evidence that another type of relation is being explicitly invoked by Gregory, namely, causal or aetiological

relations. Many modern trinitarian theologies lack an aetiology sufficiently sophisticated as to enable an appreciation or critique of patristic trinitarian theologies: this is especially true for any reading of Gregory's trinitarian theology. It is clear from the foregoing citation of Gregory, for example, that it would be a crude reduction of his aetiology to think that differences among God's products require different divine powers or productive capacities.

27 See my *The Power of God: Δύναμις in Gregory of Nyssa's Trinitarian Theology* (Washington, DC: Catholic University of America Press, 2001).

28 It is interesting to note that while Augustine (in *Sermon* 52) explicitly rejects the use of analogy (which he even defines) for understanding the Trinity, Gregory uses the term— and the process—regularly.

29 *On the Making of Mankind* XVI.11, NPNF V:405. The same doctrine occurs in the later *Catechetical Oration*: "For He who made man for the participation of His own peculiar good, and incorporated in him the instincts for all that was excellent, in order that his desire might be carried forward by a corresponding movement in each case to its like, would never have deprived him of that most excellent and precious of all goods; I mean the gift implied in being his own master, and having a free will. For if necessity in any way was the master of the life of man, the 'image' would have been falsified in that particular part, by being estranged owing to this unlikeness to its archetype. How can that nature which is under a yoke and bondage to any kind of necessity be called an image of a Master Being? Was it not, then, most right that that which is in every detail made like the Divine should possess in its nature a self-ruling and independent principle, such as to enable the partici-pation of good to be the reward of its virtue?" *Cat Or.* V, NPNF V:479.

30 There is an old point of controversy in scholarship over the character of the difference, according to Gregory, between our will and that of the angels.

31 Although it is not possible in this article to develop the following two observation, none-theless we can note: (1) Gregory's remark that whatever is "the result of compulsion and force cannot be virtue" figures in his and Gregory of Nazianzus' insistence—over against Athanasius'—that the Son is generated by the Father not only "by nature" but also "by will". This is another example of the connection between Gregory's psychology and his theology of the Trinity; (2) This emphasis on freedom means that Gregory is suspicious of "mission" language being applied to the Son and Spirit. Eunomius emphasizes the servant-status of the Son, and the polemical context militates against Gregory countenancing any related language. See *Against Eunomius' Creed of 383*, NPNF V:132.

32 Even to get as far as saying that *both the Son and Holy Spirit have a "free will"* leaves open the question, "*Free* because—like us—*in the image of* Free Will, or *free* because possessing freedom itself?"

33 *The Catechetical Oration of St. Gregory of Nyssa*, J. H. Srawley, trans. (London: SPCK, 1903). p. 26 n. 1. Srawley's translation of *The Catechetical Oration* is the best in English, but the NPNF edition is infinitely more available. The critical edition of E. Mühlenberg, GNO I.iv may be readily found in *Discours Catéchétique*, Raymond Winling, intro., trans., and comm., Sources Chrétiennes 453 (Paris: Les Éditions du Cerf, 2000).

34 Much has been made lately of the significance of the term "prosopon" (πρόσωπον) in Gregory's trinitarian theology, but that significance has been overstated. The term is important only for Gregory's early writings, and as his theology continued to mature he places less and less weight on it. Sometime ago Stead showed how Gregory's substantial use of πρόσωπον was specific to *Ad Graecos* (especially) and *Ep.* 38, and that the term occurred only rarely in *de Trin.* and *On "Not Three Gods"*. [See Christopher Stead, "Why Not Three Gods? The Logic of Gregory of Nyssa's Trinitarian Doctrine", *Studien zu Gregor von Nyssa und der Christlichen Spätanike*, Hubertus Drobner and Christoph Klock, eds (Leiden: E. J. Brill, 1990), pp. 149–162.] πρόσωπον makes no significant appearance in the *Great Catechism*, where Gregory has an extended account of the real, separate existences of the Word and the Spirit. The early importance of πρόσωπον for Gregory seems likely to have been something he inherited from Basil, and, like his brother, Gregory felt the need to separate the term from its use by Marcellus of Ancyra. ("Sabellianism" enters into the polemic as a code name for Marcellus and his modalism.)

35 Although an example from Origen is somewhat anachronistic, it does illustrate an alternative: "… the Christ, on the basis of our previous investigation, will be understood to be the 'Word'—although the reason which is in us has no individuality [περιγραφή] apart

from us—possessing substance [ὑπόστασις] 'in the beginning', that is in wisdom." Origen, *Commentary on Gospel According to John* I.292, Ronald J. Heine, trans. and comm., Fathers of the Church vol. 80 (Washington, DC, Catholic University of America Press, 1989), p. 94.

36 For a clear description of the traditional understandings of ὑπόστασις in the first half of the fourth century, see Joseph Lienhard, "The 'Arian' Controversy: Some Categories Reconsidered", *Theological Studies*, XLVIII (1987), pp. 415–436.

37 I am, however, willing to say that the terms probably entered the tradition originally (with Origen and Tertullian) because of their available connotations. It is important to be clear that initial (early third century) motivation is not necessarily identical with the later (second-half fourth century) motivation: for the fourth century the drive is tradition and existing preference(s) of expression.

38 This is the case as well among those who—without supporting Nicaea—opposed the theology which had developed in opposition to that council (e.g., Basil of Ancyra).

39 The theological priority of essence language in Nicene theology was the basis of Harnack's judgment of the "fall" from Nicaea, 325, to Constantinople, 381.

40 A hard-edged Nicene like Marcellus of Ancyra could object to any use of "two" when speaking of the divinity: all important assertions about God were to be made using only the singular.

41 For more on this, see my "The Fourth Century as Trinitarian Canon", *Theology, Rhetoric and Community*, Studies in Christian Origins, vol. I, L. Ayres and G. Jones, eds (London & New York: Routledge, 1997), pp. 47–67.

42 I have referred to this argument previously, namely that since the Father, Son, and Holy Spirit can be shown to possess the same power (δύναμις), then they must have the same nature. What Gregory does is to argue that if we can identify certain attributes as belonging exclusively to the divine, and we can show that the Son and Spirit possess this attribute, then we can conclude that the Son and Spirit must then be divine also.

43 The "invariable character of the nature"—τὸ ἀπαράλλακτον τῆς φύσεως—is a technical phrase, used often by Basil of Caesarea (and, at one point in his career, Athanasius), to say what later is said by ὁμοούσιος. Thus Gregory is beginning by saying, "While we confess unity...."

44 Most English translations of this passage (such as that in the NPNF) have the word "person" here, but "person"—ὑπόστασις—does not actually appear in this sentence, and is rather carried over from the previous sentence as the implied referent. The Greek is "τὸ ἕτερον τοῦ ἑτέρου", a phrase with few pretensions.

45 GNO III.1.56.3–10, NPNF V:336, edited, and with emphasis added.

46 Strangely, this use of "uncaused" as the criterion of divinity is something that Eunomius had in common with some Nicenes (much to their horror).

47 Father is not Son, but Father *is* Father *of* Son.

48 An important late-fourth-century Greek work against these two modalists is the so-called *Fourth Oration*, in the past attributed to Athanasius (and included in the NPNF volume for that saint).

49 Impugning the *divinity* of the Son, yes; the separate existence or reality of the Son, no.

50 *Oration* XXX.vi, NPNFVII:319.

51 The most metaphysical description Nazianzus can offer is to describe the Spirit in language which has to do with *soul*: "... He acts and says such and such things, and defines, and is grieved, and is angered, and has all the qualities which belong clearly to *one that moves.*" "Movement" here is of an interior kind.

52 *Catechetical Oration* II, NPNF V:477, Winling, *Discours Catéchétique*, 154.20–21.

53 *Catechetical Oration* II, NPNF V:477, Winling, *Discours Catéchétique*, 154.30–34.

54 "... δύναμίς τις οὐσιώδης καθ' ἑαυτὴν ὑφεστῶσα καὶ τὸ δοκοῦν ἐργαζόμενη δι' αὐτεξουσίου κινήματος." GNO I.99.8–9. The NPNF gives "A certain essential power, self-subsisting, which works its will by a spontaneous impulse", which, first, begs the question of what an "essential power" is, and, second, makes the last clause sound much more psychological— i.e., cognitive volition—than the Greek supports. See NPNF V:57.

55 Written possibly as much as five years later than the *Against Eunomius*.

56 In this case, "an existent Power possessing an individual existence, an individual".

57 In this case, "with a faculty of moral choice, self-moved, active, always choosing what is good, and for its every purpose having a power sufficient to its will".

58 The term "power" is not sufficient in itself, for it leaves open a use like Philo's, in which the powers have only a derivative existence.

59 If the Spirit, like the Son, is an "Individual with a faculty of a moral choice", it would be possible, in logic, to describe something as an "individual with no faculty of a moral choice".

60 The older Stoic sense of προαίρεσις, by contrast, had the term relegated to being a kind of preparatory choice, a "choice before a choice", For a contextual definition of προαίρεσις which makes clear its importance and technical character, see Brad Inwood, *Ethics and Human Action in Early Stoicism* (Oxford: Clarendon Press, 1985), pp. 240–242. It is Inwood who suggests the translation of προαίρεσις as "moral personality". See also Albrecht Dihle, *The Theory of Will in Classical Antiquity*, pp. 60–61, especially his fulsome footnote 49, on p. 193. Winling, *Discours Catechétique*, also recognizes the technical sense of Gregory's use of προαίρεσις.

61 I summarized the psychological phenomenology described in *On the Soul and Resurrection* as: the will is ineffective in its attachment to the good; this lack of effectiveness is due to what is experienced as a conflict in the will; and this conflict suggests divisions in the will, i.e., the will is not meaningfully one with itself.

62 *Catechetical Oration* I, NPNF V:476, Winling, *Discours Catechétique*, 148.48–60.

63 See *On First Principles* I.II.6.

64 See my *The Power of God*, Chapter Six, "The Pro-Nicene Doctrine of Divine Productivity."

65 This emphasis in doctrine undoubtedly comes from more than just fourth-century Trinitarian theology. Manichaeism, which Gregory criticizes regularly, may be said to have had a doctrine of the insufficiency of the will of the Good. In any direct confrontation between good and evil, evil wins; the good can only run away to fight (or run away again) another day.

66 As, for example, in *Cat. Or.* V, "Now in what has been previously said, the Word of God has been shown not to be this actual utterance of speech, or the possession of some science or art, but to be a power essentially and substantially existing, *willing all good, and being possessed of strength to execute all its will*; and, of a world that is good, this power appetitive and creative of good is the cause." NPNF V:478, emphasis added.

67 "It was … shown that the Word of God is a substantial and individually existent being, Himself both God and the Word; Who has embraced in Himself all creative power, or rather *Who is very power with an impulse to all good; Who works out effectually whatever He wills by having a power concurrent with His will*; Whose will and work is the life of all things that exist…." *Cat. Or.* VIII, NPNF V:484, emphasis added.

68 This passage is given in the previous footnote.

69 In her translation of *On the Soul and the Resurrection* Catharine P. Roth inserts a footnote to express her shock at Gregory's description of Moses' moral perfection. See her *On the Soul and the Resurrection* (Crestwood, NY: St. Vladimir's Seminary Press, 1993), p. 52 n. 8.

70 This feature of Gregory's moral psychology is very much in keeping with the Stoic notion of the sage, which Gregory otherwise seems to employ (or be influenced by). In the *Life of Macrina* Gregory's sister is repeatedly praised as the "true philosopher", and several scholars have noted the resemblance between Gregory's portrait of Macrina and Stoic biographies of sages.

71 Gregory's doctrine of "universal salvation" should not be taken to mean that in this lifetime everyone will become pure of heart and see, in interior vision, God reflected in us. Gregory says clearly that the degree of our purification in this lifetime affects our knowledge of God in the next: it determines where we "start from" in our spiritual movement towards God. See his *On the Premature Death of Infants*.

72 There was in Stoicism a *topos* on the inability of any two individuals to "do" the same act—an act being defined from intention to performance, so the question is a philosophical issue at the time, inherited from Stoic analysis. Augustine is more explicitly and substantially engaged with the Stoic *topos* than Gregory, and thus his shock at the fact of the Trinity's unity of wills is all the greater—a shock which is, of course, supported by other elements of his anthropology. Augustine is adamant that no human obtains to psychological integrity in this life—he explicitly denies this of cases like Moses and anyone said to live an "angelic life"—and thus the individual integrity of the will of each Individual in the Trinity, as well as the communal integrity of the wills, is all the more wondrous, divine, and

66   *Michel René Barnes*

"other". While it is true that Gregory's discursive (or linguistic) sense of God's otherness is greater, Augustine has a greater existential sense of God's otherness.

73   A passage from Gregory of Nazianzus' *Oration XXIX*.12 well illustrates the reality of this Trinitarian "common will": "For what, says He, is the Will of My Father? That everyone that believeth on the Son should be saved, and obtain the final Resurrection. Now is this the Will of the Father, but not of the Son? Or does He preach the Gospel, and receive men's faith against His will? Who could believe that? ... For I cannot see how that which is common to two can be said to belong to one alone, however much I consider it, and I do not think any one else can." NPNF VII:314.

74   One very specialized question thus emerges: in what way does the unity of humanity, by which is meant humanity as the "first creation", provide the basis for a unified willing among what is, after all, "one human"? (I am here invoking Gregory's doctrine of the "two-stage creation" of humanity as given, e.g., in *On the Nature of Humanity* and the *Catechetical Oration*.)

75   *Against Eunomius' Creed of 383*, NPNF V:132, GNO II.403.4–7. Other than in the phrase "community of will", each occurrence of "will" is βουλή. Note the parallel use of "κοινωνια" for nature and will. (The NPNF gives this work as book II of Gregory's *Against Eunomius*, but it has been established for some time that this book is a separate work.)

76   Or, alternately conceived, we can say that the individuality of the wills does no "work" in Gregory's trinitarian theology, except (perhaps) in discussions of the Father's production of the Son and Spirit. But even there, the conceptual link between divine will and divine nature leaves the individuality ambiguous. See, for example, these two passages from *Against Eunomius* III.6 (which the NPNF calls "Book VIII"): "For *the good and the eternal will is contemplated as operating, indwelling, and co-existing in the eternal Nature*, not arising in it from any separate principle, nor capable of being conceived apart from the object of will ..." and "... in the case of that Nature which is unspeakable and above all thought, our apprehension of all comes together simultaneously-of the eternal existence of the Father, and of an *act of will* concerning the Son, and of the Son Himself...." NPNF V:202–03, emphasis added.

77   *On "Not Three Gods"*, NPNF V:335.

78   *Oration XXX*.12, NPNF VII:314.

79   I want to acknowledge the contribution of what might be described as conceptual "reverse lend-lease" from Lewis Ayres, and, similarly, to thank Susan Needham for her editorial works of supererogation.

4

DIVINE TRANSCENDENCE AND HUMAN TRANSFORMATION: GREGORY OF NYSSA'S ANTI-APOLLINARIAN CHRISTOLOGY

BRIAN E. DALEY, S.J.

It is something of a commonplace among historians of early Christian doctrine to say that Gregory of Nyssa's portrait of the person of Christ is both puzzling and unsatisfactory. Puzzling, because it does not easily fit into the taxonomy of fifth-century controversy, or take a clear position within the categories of nature and person—οὐσία and φύσις, ὑπόστασις and πρόσωπον —which Gregory himself helped define for the Trinitarian mystery, and which were to be canonized for Christology during the debate around Chalcedon. Unsatisfactory, because Gregory seems—sometimes even in the same sentence—to combine the features of both a fundamentally unitive and a fundamentally divisive Christology, the spectres of Nestorianism and Eutychianism, in a single rather unsophisticated vision. Tixeront, writing early this century, speaks for many since his time when he writes:

> In several passages (Gregory) … seems to distinguish two persons in Jesus: the man, in the Savior, is a tabernacle where the Word dwells; the divinity is in Him who suffers. (*Contra Eunomium* III, 3, 51 (GNO II/2 (Leiden, 1960), p. 126); *ibid*. 62 (130); *Antirrheticus adversus Apollinarium* 54 (GNO III/I (Leiden, 1958) 222f.)). However, the contrary tendency—the Monophysite tendency—is more striking and at times makes us feel somewhat uneasy.[1]

Tixeront goes on to explain that this uneasiness is mainly inspired by Gregory's frequent use of the terminology of *mixture* to describe the relation of the divine and the human in Christ, and by his insistence that the

Brian E. Daley, S.J.
University of Notre Dame, Department of Theology, 346 Malloy Hall, Notre Dame, IN 46556, USA

humanity of Jesus was gradually transformed by the dominant power of the divine nature, so that in the end—like a drop of vinegar in a boundless ocean—it is virtually unrecognizable, swallowed up in the greatness of God.[2] For Tixeront, such conflicting tendencies are typical of the "obscurities" of fourth-century Greek Christological language, which had still not reached the level of professional precision needed to "bring the Christological problem to a perfectly satisfactory and definite solution"—a consummation, presumably, that in his view would begin with Leo's *Tome*, and reach its full development in Western scholasticism.[3]

It is my contention here that if one considers Gregory of Nyssa's theological portrait of Christ in its own terms—within the characteristic features of his thought and style, and within the context of the controversies that exercised him in his own day—one will find it remarkably powerful and also remarkably consistent, both in itself and with the rest of his thought on God, creation, and the mystery of salvation. Gregory never treats of the person and being of Christ in a single, thematically focussed treatise, comparable to his *opuscula* on the Trinity; most of his Christological writing appears either in a polemical context—in works against Eunomian Arianism or the "new" heresy of the Apollinarians—or in works dealing with the interior, spiritual fulfilment of the individual, such as *On Perfection* or the *Commentary on the Song of Songs*. Surprisingly, perhaps, he rarely uses the vocabulary he and his fellow Cappadocians had so carefully honed for Trinitarian discussions to express what is one and what is manifold in Christ, but speaks instead in a variety of scriptural and philosophical images which were richly suggestive for him, but which were used for different purposes by both sides of the Christological conflicts a half-century later.

Perhaps the simplest way to characterize what is distinctive in Gregory's Christology in a brief paper such as this is to consider the main lines of the conception of Christ's person and work that he developed in controversy with the Apollinarians, a group he charged with being even more wrongheaded and dangerous than Eunomius and the later Arians.[4] Gregory's first work directed against this ambitious and theological creative new ecclesiastical party was probably his letter addressed to Theophilus, bishop of Alexandria, shortly after the latter's election in 385. In it, Gregory asks for the help of Theophilus and his clergy in resisting the missionary activities of the Apollinarians. Their position, he says somewhat over-simply, is to "represent the Word and creator of the ages, the Son of Man, as fleshly, and divinity of the Son as mortal"—a summary of Apollinarian Christology that also characterizes his interpretation of it in the longer *Antirrhetikos*.[5] But his main effort in this brief letter is to refute the main Apollinarian charge against him and his colleagues: that by insisting on the completeness of Jesus' humanity, including a human consciousness or νοῦς, they are teaching "two Sons …, one who is so by nature, the other who has become so later by appointment".[6]

In reply, Gregory presents the Incarnation of the Word as the culmination of the theophanies of sacred history—all acts of self-revelation by a single divine Son. Since the previous appearances of the Son had not had the desired effect of communicating the fullness of the divine reality for the healing of a fallen, ever-more-fleshly humanity, "he emptied himself, so that nature might receive as much of him as it could hold".[7] As in the treatise *On Perfection*, where human salvation and fulfilment are conceived as the process of coming to be like Christ, sharing all his moral and spiritual characteristics, through a combination of intimate, contemplative knowledge and disciplined imitation,[8] Gregory assumes here that the saving process begins in the revelation of the glory of God, and that the Son has achieved this in a new and unparalleled way in his life, death and resurrection, by the moral and physical transformation of weak human flesh. The real news of the Gospel, Gregory suggests here, is that the Word, who remains transcendent and unchanging, has taken on human nature in the man Jesus and made it his own, so that "everything that was weak and perishable in our nature, mingled with the Godhead, has become that which the Godhead is".[9]

The point of the Incarnation, in other words, is that the human nature of Jesus, as the "first fruits" of a redeemed humanity, should gradually lose the distinguishing characteristics (ἰδιώματα) of our fallen race—corruptibility, mortality, the capacity to change for the worse—and take on the characteristics of the divine nature, "absorbed by the omnipotent divinity like a drop of vinegar mingled in the boundless sea".[10] Gregory clearly has in mind the manifestations of the risen Lord, who has passed through the trials of weakness and death and has received, in and for his humanity, "the name above every name" (Phil. 2.9), his own eternal titles of "Lord" and "Christ" (Acts 2:36):[11]

> For a duality of Sons might consistently be presumed, if a nature of a different kind could be recognized by its own proper signs within the ineffable Godhead of the Son ... But since all the traits we recognize in the mortal (Jesus) we see transformed by the characteristics of the Godhead, and no difference of any kind can be perceived—for whatever one sees in the Son is Godhead: wisdom, power, holiness, freedom from passivity—how could one divide what is single ...?[12]

There is no danger, in other words, of the kind of Christological dualism the Apollinarians fear, provided one sees that the man Jesus, "taken up" by the eternal Son, is constantly being transformed in role and character to reveal the Son ever more fully in himself.

This same approach to the relationship of Christ's humanity and divinity underlies the more elaborate argument in Gregory's longer anti-Apollinarian polemic, the *Antirrhetikos*. This tract, which seems to have been written somewhat later than the *Letter to Theophilus*,[13] is a phrase-by-phrase analysis and rebuttal of Apollinarius's *Demonstration of the Divine Incarnation in*

Human Likeness (Apodeixis), a work for which Gregory's quotations are now virtually our only source. Here Apollinarius apparently accuses his opponents of holding that Christ is simply a divinely inspired human being, an ἄνθρωπος ἔνθεος,[14] and that the crucified saviour had "nothing divine in his own nature".[15] By rejecting his party's conception of Christ as the divine mind enfleshed in an animated body, Apollinarius argues, his opponents' only alternative is to conceive of him as a graced human being:

> If the Lord is not enfleshed mind (νοῦς ἔνσαρκος), he must be wisdom enlightening the mind of a human being; but that is in all people. And if that is so, then the coming of Christ was not the presence of God (ἐπιδημία θεοῦ), but the birth of a human being.[16]

For Apollinarius, the elements of the Saviour can only be the eternal divine Mind or Spirit and the animal body of "flesh" he assumed: "He is God in virtue of the enfleshed Spirit, and human in virtue of the flesh taken on by God."[17] And since his fleshly component is not "foreign" to the divine Spirit—as it would be if it "belonged" to a human mind as part of a complete human being[18]—it is accurate, in Apollinarius's view, even to say that "Christ the human being" is heavenly and eternal:

> The human being Christ pre-exists, not in that the Spirit—that is, God—is another alongside him, but in that the Lord in the nature of the God-man is the Divine Spirit.[19]

When one looks beneath the conventional rhetorical surface of his response, Gregory's critique of Apollinarius is based on a distinctively different understanding of both the being of God and the nature of salvation.

> "Who does not know", he asks scornfully, "that the God revealed to us in flesh, according to the word of pious tradition, is immaterial and invisible and uncompounded, and that he was and is infinite and uncircumscribed, existing everywhere and penetrating all creation, but that he has been seen, as far as appearance goes, in human circumscription?"[20]

Apollinarius's conception of Christ not only limits the Logos by making him the rational soul or "spirit" guiding a human body;[21] it implies that this one governing soul, at least, is eternal, σύμφυλον θεοῦ.[22] Secondly, Gregory insists, to replace the human mind of Christ with the eternal Logos is to make his humanity simply into a lower form of animal life, a "beast of burden";[23] to have a right to be called human and to be the revealer of human ἀρετή, Christ needed a human mind, human needs and limitations, and especially a human will.[24]

This last point is of central importance for Gregory's own understanding of the person and work of Christ. The message of Scripture about Jesus, Gregory says, is that "the divine being, changeless and unvarying in essence, has come to be in a changeable and alterable nature, so that by his own unchangeability he might heal our tendency to change for the worse."[25] So it is essential for him to conceive of Christ the Saviour as possessing all that is vulnerable and variable in our nature, including our mind, precisely so that all of what is natural and changeable in each of us may, beginning in Christ, be transformed and exalted.[26] The κένωσις of the Son, spoken of in Phil. 2:7, is not simply another revelation of the eternal God in our changeable world, Gregory argues, but the concrete act of God, at a definite point in our history, taking on a human being as something new, but thoroughly his own.[27] So Gregory insists quite simply that the eternal "Christ" and "Lord" in the course of time "took up a man"[28]—"not purely and simply a common man",[29] since he was born by a divine mode of conception, yet certainly a man in the full sense;[30] and the salvation he has worked for all humanity is nothing less than to have transformed the passible, corruptible characteristics (ἰδιώματα) of that man into the divine characteristics of the Son, so that in his exaltation the man can now share the "name that is above every name"—the eternal, unnameable reality of God.[31] As a result, the believer always *knows* Jesus Christ in two ways, both as a human being and as God—"human in what is seen, God in what is known to the mind".[32]

Towards the end of the *Antirrhetikos*, in a passage of striking clarity, Gregory sums up the relationship between the eternal Son—who is himself always called "Christ" and "Lord" because he is always anointed by the Spirit and ruler over all creation[33]—and the human being he has assumed:

We say that he is always the Christ, both before the economy and after it; but he is human neither before it nor after it, but only during the time of the economy. For the flesh, in its own proper characteristics (ἰδιώμασιν) did not exist before the Virgin, nor after his ascent into heaven. "For even if we once knew Christ according to the flesh", Scripture says, "we no longer know him thus" (II Cor. 5:16) ... But since humanity is changeable, but the divine unchangeable, the divinity is not moveable by alteration, either towards the better or towards the worse (since it does not receive what is worse and there is nothing which is better); but the human nature in Christ does possess the ability to change for the better, being transformed from corruption to incorruption, from what is perishable to what is imperishable, from what is short-lived to what is eternal, from what is bodily and of perceptible shape to what is bodiless and without shape.[34]

The importance of this transformation in Christ, for Gregory, is of course that it marks the beginning of the transformation in which each of us is called to participate: a transformation of the human into the divine which does not seem to involve, in his view, an annihilation of human nature, so much as the suffusion of all its naturally changeable, "fleshly" characteristics with the stability and luminous vigour of God. Both ἕνωσις, after all, and the various terms for "mixture" which Gregory habitually employs for the union

in Christ (μίξις, κρᾶσις and their cognates), mean in his vocabulary the close
unification of elements that still remain naturally or numerically *different*: a
relationship (σχέσις) rather than a total absorption.[35] Unlike Aristotle, who
uses the image of a drop of wine in ten thousand gallons of water as an
example of the kind of mixture that annihilates the smaller element
altogether,[36] Gregory seems to see even the lesser, human partner in the
"mixture" of the Incarnation—though absorbed now like the proverbial drop
of vinegar in the ocean of divinity and no longer perceptible, through any of
its own peculiar qualities, to mind or sense[37]—as continuing to exist and
even to undergo further change. And as the "first-fruits" of a new humanity,
endlessly undergoing transformation into the qualities that reflect the stable
glory of God, the risen and transfigured human Christ is the one means by
which the rest of the race can also participate in that same process of
"divinization": not, be it said, through some connection conceived of in
purely physical terms, or through sharing in some Platonic universal,[38] but
through human involvement with Christ in salvation history, especially
through faith, baptism, and a disciple's imitation.[39]

Gregory's anti-Apollinarian Christology, as we have briefly sketched it
out here, is certainly strange, even a little shocking, by post-Chalcedonian
standards. The reason, I would suggest, is first of all terminological. The
language of φύσις and ὑπόστασις, οὐσία and πρόσωπον, which were to
frame the debates of the fifth and sixth centuries and which had been given
stable definition for Trinitarian discussion by the Cappadocians themselves,
are strikingly absent, as I have already said, from Gregory's discussion of
Christ; both ὑπόστασις and πρόσωπον, in fact, when they are used in these
works, are applied to the man Jesus alone, not to the incarnate Christ.[40] The
reason, presumably, is that Gregory is afraid to support the Apollinarian
conception of the man Jesus as ἓν πρόσωπον and ἓν ζῶον with the eternal
hypostasis of the Son; such terms are too multivalent within the theological
realm of discourse, too analogous, to be used safely in the same context
of both the "persons" of the Trinity and a human person, of both the
"substance" of God and our human reality.

In any case, Gregory's Christology differs from that of the fifth-century
debates also in that his main interest is *not* to identify precisely what is one
and what is manifold in Christ, but to explore the conditions of possibility
for our sharing in his triumph over death and human corruption. Not only is
the modern category of "person", as autonomous and reflective subject, far
from his mind, as it was from that of all the Greek Fathers; his real interest
is in our salvation: in what happens to human *nature*—to τὸ ἀνθρώπινον, the
common reality all of us concretely share—when it is brought into contact
with τὸ θεῖον, the transcendent reality of God, through the one historical
individual who is, in an unconfused and inseparable way, both God and
a human being. Nonetheless, it is clear that for him, as for the classical
Christology of the fifth, sixth and seventh centuries, the Mystery of Christ is

also one of unconfused and undivided union: God the Word making a complete human being his own instrument of revelation and healing for the world, while at the same time enabling that human being to be, most perfectly, what all humans are created to be—fully itself, and fully, though always increasingly, a participant in the life and even the qualities of God.

In a recent, thoughtful article comparing Origen's *De Principiis* and Gregory's *Catechetical Oration* as synthetic constructions of Christian theology, Anthony Meredith remarks: "By and large, Origen's thought is largely theocentric, Gregory's is Christocentric."[41] The reason, Meredith suggests, is Gregory's preoccupation with Apollinarianism. While I would certainly agree on the central place given to the person and work of Christ in all Gregory's thought, I suggest that he is not concerned with *Christology* in the same sense or to the same degree as Nestorius, Cyril, Theodoret and Leo would be, let alone Severus, Leontius of Byzantium and Maximus Confessor. He is concerned above all with Jesus Christ as the man in whom and through whom the infinite and saving reality of God touches us all: with preserving the transcendence of the God who is present in him, and with emphasizing the transformation of that human reality which God, in the man Jesus, has made his own.

NOTES

1 J. Tixeront, *Histoire des dogmes dans l'antiquité chrétienne* II (Paris, 1912), p. 128 (Eng. trans.: *History of Dogmas* II (St. Louis, 1914), p. 127). Here, as elsewhere in this paper, I have cited Gregory of Nyssa's works by referring to the critical edition, *Gregorii Nysseni Opera* (GNO) (Leiden, 1958–).

2 Ibid.; Tixeront cites *Ctr. Eun.* III, 3, 34 (GNO II/2, 119); 44 (123); 63 (130); 67 (131); *Antirrh.* 42 (GNO III/1, 201). Tixeront might also have cited, as evidence for Gregory's paradoxical Christological language, a passage in *Antirrhetikos* 48, in which Gregory is discussing Apollinarius's tendency to speak of Christ, the "heavenly man", as composed of the three irreducible elements of body, soul and spirit. "To some degree", Gregory writes, "we do not disagree with him; for in saying that all the elements comprising our nature are also found in that man, one would not be wrong. 'But the heavenly man, too', he says of the Lord, 'is also a life-giving spirit'. This, too, we accept ... For the one mingled with the heavenly man, who transformed his earthly element through blending it with what is superior to it, is no longer called earthly but heavenly." For an interpretation stressing rather the similarity of Gregory's Christology to that of the Antiochene school, see J. N. D. Jelly, *Early Christian Doctrines* (5th ed.: San Francisco, 1976), pp. 298–300.

3 Ibid., p. 130 (Eng. trans. 129f.); cf. 126 (Eng. trans. 126): "The terminology of our authors (in the fourth century) was not sufficiently accurate, nor their conception of the doctrine sufficiently precise, to enable them to bring to a successful issue that work which was to be the work, not of mere witnesses of the tradition, but of professional and well-trained theologians, working on the data of tradition." For a more nuanced judgment on Gregory's Christology, which nevertheless still judges it confused and inadequate, precisely in judging it by Chalcedonian standards, see A. Grillmeier, *Christ in Christian Tradition* I (London and Oxford, 1975), pp. 371f., 376.

4 *Antirrh.* 44 (GNO III/1, 205.21–206.9).

5 *Ad Theophilum adversus Apollinaristas* (GNO III/1, 120.14f.). For this same interpretation of Apollinarian Christology in Gregory's contemporaries, see below, n. 22.

6 Ibid. (120.17f.).

74   Brian E. Daley

7   Ibid. (123.7–14).
8   GNO VIII/1, 173–214, esp. 205.22–206.14.
9   Ibid. (126.10f.).
10 Ibid. (126.19f.).
11 Ibid. (127.12f.). These two texts are part of a small group of New Testament passages Gregory repeatedly uses, throughout his writings, to construct his theory of the continuing identity of the Word within the saving transformation of the human being he assumed. Besides the full text of the "hymn to Christ" in Phil. 2:5–11, they include John 20:17 (the risen Christ telling his disciples, through Mary Magdalene, "I am ascending to my Father and to your Father, to my God and to your God"); the parable of the lost sheep (Lk. 15:4f.), in which humanity is seen as the strayed sheep "taken up" by the word; and the combination of the images of humanity as "mass" of dough (Matt. 13:33) and the risen Christ as the "first-fruits" of a new humanity (I Cor. 15:23). See the thorough discussions of Lucas F. Mateo-Seco, *Estudios sobre la cristología de san Gregorio de Nisa* (Pamplona, 1978), esp. pp. 30–74 (Phil. 2:5–11); and Reinhard M. Hübner, *Die Einheit des Leibes Christi bei Gregor von Nyssa. Untersuchungen zum Ursprung der "physischen" Erlösungslehre* (Leiden, 1974), esp. pp. 104–145.
12 Ibid., (126.21–127.9).
13 So G. May, "Die Chronologie des Lebens und des Werkes Gregors von Nyssa", in M. Harl (ed), *Ecriture et culture philosophique dans la pensée de Grégoire de Nysse* (Colloquium of Chevetogne, 1969) (Leiden, 1971), p. 61, following H. Lietzmann, *Apollinarius von Laodicaea und seine Schule I* (Tübingen, 1904), p. 83f. and E. Mühlenberg, *Apollinarius von Laodicaea* (Göttingen, 1969), p. 90. The main arguments for putting the *Antirrhetikos* later than the letter to Theophilus are the letter's total lack of reference to the arguments of the longer work, and the fact that Gregory of Nazianzus does not seem to have known about Apollinarius's *Apodeixis* before the mid-380s. J. Daniélou, "La chronologie des œuvres de Grégoire de Nysse", *Studia Patristica* 7 (TU 92: Berlin, 1966), p. 163f., suggests the *Antirrhetikos* was composed in the winter of 382–383, on the basis of the work's treatment of the relation of the Logos to Jesus' soul and body in death; in this dating he follows J. Lebourlier, "A propos de l'état du Christ dans la mort, II", *Revue des sciences philosophiques et théologiques* 47 (1963), p. 180, and is joined by Hübner, p. 135f., n. 166. The chronology of Gregory's works is a notoriously speculative business.
14 *Antirrh.* 4 (GNO III/1, 135.17–24); cf. 25 (169.21ff.).
15 Ibid., 27 (172.16ff.).
16 Ibid., 36 (188.23–27).
17 Ibid., 7 (140.3ff.). It is interesting to note the frequent echoes, in the passages of Apollinarius's *Apodeixis* quoted by Gregory, of the "Spirit-Christology" of the second and third centuries: drawing on I Cor. 15:45 ("the second Adam is a life-giving spirit"), Gregory notes, Apollinarius "says he is called '(the man) from heaven' for this reason, that the heavenly spirit is made flesh in him". (Ibid., 12 (146.27f.)). See also Apollinarius's epistle to Jovianus 1 (Lietzmann 250.7, 251.15). On "Spirit-Christology" in the Patristic period, see M. Simonetti, "Note di cristologia pneumatica", *Augustini-anum* 12 (1972), pp. 210–232; G. W. H. Lampe, *God as Spirit* (Oxford, 1977), pp. 210–227.
18 Ibid., 22 (162.17–19).
19 Ibid., 12 (147.12ff.).
20 Ibid., 18 (156.14–18).
21 Ibid., (156.26–157.9); 35 (185.7–10). Cf. 50 (227.23–26): "If human nature receives either a mind like ours or God in place of a mind, these two must be of the same magnitude and status as each other—if indeed the place where mind is contained is also the place where divinity is received."
22 Ibid., 28 (174.14–19). It is in the context of his insistence that the identification of the divine Logos with a νοῦς capable of governing a human composite is a violation of the divine transcendence that one should probably understand Gregory's oft-repeated point— exaggerated, surely, for rhetorical purposes—that Apollinarius holds even the "flesh" of Christ to be eternal (e.g., 13 (147.16–148.4); 15 (150.10ff.); 18 (155.25–156.1)). Apollinarius himself seems rather to have suggested simply that the heavenly origin of the Word implies the heavenly character of the whole Christ (see *De Unione* 1f. (Lietzmann 185f.)), stressing the Biblical image of Christ as "the Son of Man who came down from heaven"

(*Antirrh.* 6 (138.18–21, 25–29)), and thus to have asserted no more than that the *whole* Christ, as θεὸς ἔνσαρκος, entered into the world through the Virgin's womb as through a "channel" (Ibid., 24 (166.14–28). In other places, Apollinarius insists that the Word took the "created garment" of his flesh from the virgin, even though it was divinely generated in her and was never a distinct organism apart from the Word: see, e.g., *De Unione* 6, 9, 13 (Leitzmann 187f., 188f., 191). The Cappadocians, however, seem to have shared their contemporaries' sense that Apollinarius really held the very flesh of Christ pre-existed in heaven: see Athanasius, *Ep. to Epictetus* 2–9 (PG 26.1052C–1065B), a passage which seems to have the Apollinarians, among others, in mind but does not mention them by name; Basil of Caesaraea, Ep. 261.2 (PG 32.969B13–972A1); Gregory Nazianzen, Ep. 101.16 (ed P. Gallay, *Sources chrétiennes* 208.42), 30 (Ibid., 48); Ep. 202.10–13 (Ibid., 90–92); cf. Ep. 102.14f. (Ibid., 79), where Gregory suggests the Apollinarian Christ has only the appearance of human flesh.

23 *Antirrh.* 23 (165.9–28). Cf. Gregory of Nazianzus, Ep. 101.34f. (S€ 208.51): "If (Jesus) is endowed with a soul, but not with a mind, how is he human? For a human being is not an animal without intelligence. Of necessity, the outward form and tabernacle would then be human, but the soul would be that of some horse or ox or some other unintelligent being; and this will be what is saved …"

24 Ibid., 31f (179.8–182.5). In other passages, too, Apollinarius explicitly rejected the notion of two wills or operations in Christ: see, e.g., Frags. 108f., from *On the Incarnate Appearance of God* (Leitzmann 232f.); Frag. 117, from the *Syllogistic Treatise against Diodore [of Tarsus] to Heraclius* (Leitzmann 235f.).

25 Ibid., 2 (133.6–9).

26 Ibid 5 (138.7–9): "… What is passible receives death, but what is beyond the reach of passion works freedom from passibility in that which is passible"; cf. 21 (160.6–161.5).

27 Ibid., 15 (151.10–21).

28 Gregory uses various forms of this expression: see, e.g., Ibid., 7 (140.23–25: ὅλον συνάπτει τὸν ἄνθρωπον); 34 (184.1–15; ἀνθρώπου πρόσληψις); 38f. (193.6–18: ἀνάληψις and πρόσληψις); 49 (215.17–21: the very word πρόσληψις implies a difference in nature).

29 Ibid., 21 (160.3–11).

30 Ibid., 22 (203.16–29); 49f. (214.19–215.25).

31 Ibid., 21 (161.13–26): "And since the man in Christ was called by a name, in the usual way, according to what is consistent with humanity, through the mysterious instruction given to the Virgin by Gabriel, and that human element was named Jesus, as we are told, but (since) the divine nature is not graspable in a name, the two have become one by mixture (διὰ τῆς ἀνακράσεως). Therefore God is called by a human name, for 'at the name of Jesus every knee shall bow', and the man comes to be beyond all naming—something characteristic of godhead, which cannot be signified by any verbal sign—so that as the exalted being comes to exist in what is lowly, the lowly takes on exalted characteristics; for just as the godhead receives the name of the man, so that which is joined, from lowliness, to the godhead comes to be above every name."

32 Ibid., 37 (191.24ff); cf. 27 (173.10–14).

33 Ibid., 52f. (220.2–221.20).

34 Ibid., 53 (222.25–223.10).

35 See esp. Ibid., 22 (161.26f.); 34 (184.27–30). For a thorough and penetrating analysis of Gregory's terminology for the union of natures in Christ, including its background in classical philosophy, see J.-R. Bouchet, "Le vocabulaire de l'union et du rapport des natures chez saint Grégoire de Nysse", *Revue thomiste* 68 (1968), pp. 533–582.

36 *De gen. et corr* 1.10 (328a27–29).

37 *Antirrh.* 42 (GNO III/1, 201.10–16); cf. the passages cited in nn. 2 and 10 above, and *Ctr. Eun.* III, 3, 68f. (GNO II.2, 133.1–4).

38 For a careful discussion and refutation of the overly literal interpretation of Gregory's idea of human solidarity and "physical" redemption found in many histories of dogma, see especially Hübner, *Die Einheit des Leibes Christi* (above, n. 11) esp. pp. 1–25 and 95–198; cf. Mateo-Seco, *Estudios* (above, n. 11), p. 53; Bouchet, "Le vocabulaire" (above, n. 35), p. 538; and A. Lieske, "Zur Theologie der Christusmystik Gregors von Nyssa", *Scholastik* 14 (1939), p. 510.

39 So, e.g., *Antirrh.* 55 (GNO III/1, 226.17–227.9: baptism as imitation of Jesus' saving and voluntary death); cf. *On Perfection* (GNO VIII/1, esp. 210.4–214.6: imitation of Christ's ἀρεταί).

40   *Antirrh.* 54 (GNO III/1, 223.11–224.5); *Ctr. Eun.* III, 3, 42 (122.25–29). For a thorough discussion of the Christology of Gregory's works *Contra Eunomium*, see now B. Pottier, *Dieu et le Christ selon Grégoire de Nysse* (Brussels, 1994).
41   "Origen's *De Principiis* and Gregory of Nyssa's *Oratio Catechetica*", *Heythrop Journal* 36 (1995), p. 8.

This essay was originally published in *Studia Patristica* Vol. 32 (1997), pp. 87–95 and is reprinted here by kind permission.

5

UNDER SOLOMON'S TUTELAGE: THE EDUCATION OF DESIRE IN THE *HOMILIES ON THE SONG OF SONGS*

MARTIN LAIRD

Recent scholarship on Gregory of Nyssa has witnessed a re-evaluation of the nature of his theory of asceticism in general and of the relationship of desire to the rational faculty in particular. The valuable contributions of Mark Hart,[1] John Behr,[2] Rowan Williams,[3] Morwenna Ludlow,[4] among others,[5] have featured largely in this project by reassessing previous assumptions regarding the anthropological foundations of Gregory's ascetical theory. The purpose of this essay is to take this re-evaluation as a point of departure. After a brief summary of the salient features of this scholarship, I wish to explore how Gregory of Nyssa approaches this so-called problem of desire in his *Homilies on the Song of Songs*. I will suggest that, while Gregory, like Origen, sees all the Solomonic books (Proverbs, Ecclesiastes, Song of Songs) contributing to the training of desire to long for God, the pedagogy of the Song of Songs focuses, unlike Origen, on exposing desire to the apophatic. Here we will see Solomon's tutelage reveal a Trinitarian strategy that attracts and inflames desire to long for the Beloved who remains, however, beyond the bride's grasp. Through exposure to paradoxes which exercise the soul, this noetic-erotic grasp is enabled to release its controlling grip and find itself in apophatic union with the Beloved.[6]

Preliminary Considerations

(A) In a perceptive re-reading of Gregory's *De virginitate* Hart redresses the tendency to read this early work of Gregory as a clear exaltation of celibacy

Martin Laird
Department of Theology and Religious Studies, Villanova University, 800 Lancaster Avenue, Villanova, PA 19085, USA

over marriage.[7] Gregory is more fundamentally concerned, argues Hart, with showing how "the soul's desire for union with God may in fact be reconciled with the needs of family and community life that arise from the body, once the truer nature of spiritual development is understood".[8] Marriage is ultimately viable for the Christian in so far as it is founded on the very quality that makes Christian celibacy viable, i.e., non attachment.[9] With respect to the ultimate goal of union with God, the problem is not properly understood in terms of marriage versus celibacy. Marriage too leads to a life of contemplation. The problem lies with desire and the concomitant struggle with attachment to lower levels of soul. Gregory does not intend "that one must never exert energy toward the satisfaction of one's needs as an animal. Rather, what is evil or base lies in the attempt by what is most divine and highest in the soul to satisfy itself in the animal side of our nature. In this movement of the soul, the body and the soul become 'mixed' or 'confused'".[10] The viability of virginity lies in the fact that virginity is ultimately a question of non-attachment. The problem with desire, therefore, is not that it is concerned with the body *per se* but that the soul seeks ultimacy in what is not God. It is a problem within the soul itself. The healing remedy is not disembodiment but rather dispassion (ἀπάθεια).[11] Hart succeeds in showing that ultimately for Gregory of Nyssa the ascetical focus is shifted away from celibate versus married to the proper training of desire, whether celibate or married.

In many ways John Behr's persuasive study of *De hominis opificio* supports what Hart's study revealed. Focusing explicitly on the anthropology contained in *De hominis opificio*, Behr shows how the first fifteen chapters of the work present a dynamic, ascensional view of creation, culminating in humanity. The basis of Gregory's "ascending perspective", Behr argues, "is the desire (ἔφεσις) which all things have for the good and the beautiful, and ultimately for God Himself".[12] Far from derailing the search for God, desire is, as it were, the homing instinct for God. "This upward movement is counterbalanced by a downward theophanic manifestation: if the mind (our rational nature) maintains its likeness to the Divine, it will adorn our body as a mirror of the mirror. If, however, human beings do not incline in their desire (ἔφεσις) towards God, but turn towards the lower levels in their lust (ἐπιθυμία), they are transformed by the shapelessness of that which should be adorned by them".[13] Behr's observation is significant, for he shows that for Gregory of Nyssa the problem with desire is not due to its involvement with body, as, for example, Stead has suggested.[14] It is the "evil husbandry of the mind" that perverts movements of soul into passions.[15] But if reason governs the movements of the soul, what might otherwise be perverted into passion becomes virtue. "Here we have a glimpse of the dignity which Gregory regards created human reality, including sexuality, called to manifest in a truly word-bearing or angelic use".[16] If desire contributes to the problem of finding union with God, it also contributes to its attainment.

Desire need not be extirpated but educated. It is not a question of ridding oneself of desire, which can devolve into lust; it is a question of desire's proper flow.

Responding to a statement made by Christopher Stead that Gregory posits a separation of reason from desire,[17] Rowan Williams examines the anthropology contained in *De anima et resurrectione* and *De hominis opificio*. According to Stead Gregory repeats "Aristotle's mistake of regarding man simply as an animal with reason added on as an extra capacity".[18] Stead reads Gregory as giving us a "picture of the human subject as a core of rationality with impulse added on …".[19] Human realization, then, would be a question of separating impulse and desire out of the rational subject's project of attaining union with God. For Williams such a reading of Gregory will not do. A close reading of *De anima et de resurrectione* and *De hominis opificio*, Williams argues, reveals that for Gregory of Nyssa the human being does not "consist of a rational core with some embarrassing additions".[20] While it is undeniable that desire poses a problem, it is likewise undeniable that it is part of the solution. For, as Williams shows, desire is part of the rational subject, "part of how mind realizes itself".[21]

Focusing primarily on eschatology, Morwenna Ludlow examines briefly yet profitably the nature of desire in Gregory's thought. Harmonizing closely with Behr, yet independent of him, she notes that desire is dynamic and malleable. It can be aligned to materialistic impulse or to the good itself; in either case it is shaped accordingly. Rather like iron, desire can be purified of its impurities.[22] In such a purified state, "the soul will naturally be attracted to God, as like is attracted to like".[23] Desire focused on God "is the deepest and most true expression of humanity".[24] While it remains true that the ideal state of desire is dispassion (ἀπάθεια), this does not mean the disappearance of desire. "Ἀπάθεια is thus not the absence of desire but freedom from any *materialistic* impulse or passion".[25]

The four studies which we have surveyed represent what might reasonably be called the *status quaestionis* on desire in Gregory of Nyssa. The value of these studies for Gregorian scholarship lies in the fact that they clearly shift the topic of desire out of a bifurcated anthropology (reason over here, desire over there) into an intrinsically unified, subtly multilevelled, and dynamic anthropology. If the human being is to attain union with God, the former scenario required that desire be rooted out. In the second scenario as presented by Hart, Behr, Williams and Ludlow, desire cannot be rooted out if divine union is to be realized; for desire is "part of how mind realizes itself".[26] Indeed one can speak of a noetic-erotic movement toward God.

Is desire to be eradicated or educated in order for the soul to attain union with God? The history of this question has been vexing and variegated.[27] Gregory of Nyssa would seem to fall clearly in the tradition of pedagogy. The very thing that presents a difficulty to soul's union with God is also part of what makes it possible and enables soul to scale the mountain of God.[28]

If passionate desire were eradicated from the search for union, there would be no union. It is precisely desire properly educated and trained that enables the bride to search for the Beloved throughout the transcendent realm into the realm of unknowing, where, at long last, she finds her Beloved in the darkness of faith.[29] For Gregory of Nyssa there is a fundamental continuity between the noetic-erotic grasp turned in on itself, and the noetic-erotic *ungrasping* that is brought transformed into the Holy of Holies, where, communing with God, it is ever dilated, ever being filled without, paradoxically, ever becoming full.[30]

But how is the tightly clenched grasp of desire pried loose, or to use Gregory's phrase, how is "passion transformed into dispassion"?[31] Only through proper training is desire capable of unclenching its fist and entering the darkness where God dwells, entering the Holy of Holies, entering the darkness of the wedding chamber. What sort of education of desire does Gregory of Nyssa envision? Taking Hart, Behr, Williams and Ludlow as a new point of departure in this regard, this essay will examine how Gregory of Nyssa sets this out in his *Homilies on the Song of Songs*.

(B) Origen states as succinctly as anyone the ambivalent nature of desire. After discussing at some length the terms *amor* (ἔρως) and *caritas* (ἀγάπη) and concluding that the terms are synonymous, he says in the prologue to his famous *Commentary on the Song of Songs*: "… we ought to understand that it is impossible for human nature not to be always feeling the passion of love for something. Everyone who has reached the age that they call puberty loves something, either less rightly when he loves what he should not, or rightly and with profit when he loves what he should love. But some people pervert this faculty of passionate love which is implanted in the human soul by the Creator's kindness".[32]

There is no such thing as human nature without this "passionate love"; far from resulting from humanity's fallen nature,[33] it has been placed within human nature out of God's loving concern. While Origen is in no way blind to the possibilities of misuse, desire can clearly be guided and educated in such a way that, despite its potential for going astray, it can be led to loving communion with God. To serve as such a pedagogue is the precise role of the Solomonic literature. Proverbs, Ecclesiastes, and especially the Song of Songs serve each in its own way to train desire.[34] It is the Song of Songs especially which cultivates in soul a desire for God. "[In the Song of Songs] Solomon[35] instills into the soul the love of things divine and heavenly, using for his purpose the figure of the Bride and Bridegroom, and teaches us that communion with God must be attained by the paths of love and desire".[36] Gregory of Nyssa is clearly heir to this Christian exegetical tradition of seeing in the Solomonic literature a well-defined pedagogy of desire.[37]

While Gregory's extended reflections on the Song of Songs can rightly be thought of as homilies and not as a commentary in the strict sense,[38] the text nevertheless bears certain resemblances to the genre of commentary. Not least among these is the way in which Homily One functions as a prologue. One of the functions of the prologue in a commentary is to provide something of a key to the whole of the work to follow.[39] Hence, it is important to consider in some detail what amounts to a prologue to Gregory's *Homilies on the Song of Songs*.[40] Before Gregory begins to comment on the first lemma of the book, "let him kiss me with the kisses of his mouth", or even on the significance of book's title, another characteristic of a commentary's prologue,[41] he gives at least two important clues to the understanding of the Song of Songs as a whole: he tells us that the Solomonic literature contains a "philosophy" and suggests that the pedagogue in this matter is the Trinity itself.

Inflaming Desire: Solomon's Philosophical Exercises

The researches of Pierre Hadot have emphasized that an important function of philosophy in the ancient world was to serve as a guide to the soul, to exercise it, train it in its fight with the passions.[42] Early on in its encounter with hellenism Christianity took on board this sense of the term, transforming it from within. By the fourth century it had become part of ascetical and exegetical vocabulary.[43] With great cultural resonance, then, does Gregory ascribe the term "philosophy" to the Solomonic literature.[44] Philosophy exercises the soul, and the guide, the trainer, the pedagogue in the soul's exercise is the Word itself,[45] exercising the soul in the manner that best suits it; for not all are at the same level of maturity: "For this reason, Proverbs teaches in one way and Ecclesiastes in another; the philosophy of the Song of Songs transcends both by its loftier teaching".[46] Whether Proverbs, Ecclesiastes or the Song of Songs, the philosophy contained in the Solomonic books excercises the noetic-erotic capacity for God.

The task of Proverbs is to train the soul "to desire virtue".[47] Focusing on the seat of desire itself (τὸ ἐπιθυμητικὸν), Gregory says that the pedagogical strategy of Proverbs does anything but attempt to extinguish desire. Rather Proverbs attempts to stir it up, inflame it by dangling before it beautiful, tantalizing images. Proverbs seeks not to destroy or indulge soul's noetic-erotic capacity to be preoccupied with corporeal things, but to train this same desire to long for the incorporeal. And so Proverbs describes Wisdom in various ways so as to attract desire to divine Beauty. As though adorned with jewels, Wisdom's right and left hands are described as bedecked with length of years and splendid glory, and the alluring fragrance of her breath is righteousness itself (Prov. 3:16). Her lips are reddened by law and mercy. Her ambling gate is even attractively praised as she walks in the pathway of righteousness (Prov. 8:20).[48] Having presented to the seat of desire this erotic description of Wisdom's body, the Solomonic training increases the seduction by showing to the youth Wisdom's bridal chamber and bestowing nuptial crowns upon him (Prov. 4:6–9), exhorting the youth never to depart from Wisdom (Prov. 6:22).

For Gregory, then, it is important to "desire as much as you can". Indeed, he says, "fall in love".[49] For when the images of Scripture become the object of desire's ardent yearning, passion is being trained to yearn for the incorporeal. "This passion (πάθος) for the incorporeal is without reproach and dispassionate (ἀπαθὲς), as Wisdom says in Proverbs when she enjoins on us to fall in love (ἔρος) with divine Beauty".[50] Anyone who has been sufficiently excercised by the philosophy contained in Proverbs, is now ready for "the philosophy contained in Ecclesiastes".[51]

The training found in Ecclesiastes is likewise specific. Whereas the philosophy contained in Proverbs exercises soul so that it can desire not corporeal things but virtue, Ecclesiastes trains desire to long for what is beyond appearance, beyond the grasp of senses. "Solomon raises beyond everything grasped by sensible perception the movement of the soul's desire towards invisible Beauty".[52]

The philosophy contained in Proverbs and Ecclesiastes exercises what Gregory calls "the passionate faculty", "the movement of soul's desire".[53] Clearly the goal of this education is not to extinguish desire but to train it by inflaming it. Once inflamed it longs for virtue and the spiritual world. However, before examining the philosophy contained in the Song of Songs and how it exercises desire in a manner very different from the pedagogy seen in Proverbs and Ecclesiastes,[54] it is important to observe the Trinitarian dynamic of the educational initiative that undergirds the *Homilies on the Song of Songs*.

Following Origen Solomon is for Gregory of Nyssa a type of Christ. When Gregory says Solomon, he does not mean Solomon of Beersheba but rather another Solomon "born from the seed of David according to the flesh".[55] It is this other Solomon, the Word, who used "Solomon as an instrument and speaks to us through his voice first in Proverbs and then in Ecclesiastes. After these two books he speaks in the philosophy set forth in the Song of Songs and shows us the ascent to perfection in an orderly fashion".[56] It is the Word, then, who is the pedagogue in the *Homilies on the Song of Songs*. The Word trains the soul to desire divine Beauty by presenting it with attractive, indeed seductive images. The effects of this stimulation Gregory describes, not unlike Origen, in the language of fire.

In her monumental study of language and symbol in Gregory of Nyssa, Mariette Canévet establishes the connection between fire-imagery and the Holy Spirit. Sent by the Word and received by the soul, the Holy Spirit inflames desire into ever greater love of God.[57] The imagery of fire which Gregory uses to describe the effects of this Solomonic pedagogy on the seat of desire should be understood as alluding to the Holy Spirit's role in the training of desire. Moreover, the obviously baptismal imagery of the opening lines addressed to the audience,[58] also underscores the presence of the Holy Spirit.[59] Whether obvious or subtle, the fundamentally Trinitarian dynamic that undergirds the education of desire in the *Homilies on the Song of Songs* characterizes not only the philosophy contained in Proverbs and Ecclesiastes that trains desire, but also the Song of Songs itself.[60]

Philosophical Exercise in the Song of Songs

Gregory states at the outset of the *Homilies on the Song of Songs* the particular quality of the words contained in the Song of Songs.[61] "Through the words of the Song the soul is escorted to an incorporeal, spiritual, and undefiled union with God".[62] In contrast to the exercises in Proverbs and Ecclesiasties, which attempt to withdraw desire from material things and fix it to the immaterial, the philosophy contained in the Song of Songs reveals an altogether different strategy: to lead the soul to union with God who is beyond the grasp of images and conceptual understanding. Likewise in contrast to the exercises of Proverbs and Ecclesiastes, it is important to note the apophatic character of the language which Gregory employs to describe the philosophy contained in the Song of Songs. Gregory says that this union (συζυγία) is incorporeal (ἀσώματον) and undefiled (ἀμόλυντον). This grouping together of negative terms, with or without the alpha-privative, is one of Gregory's standard apophatic motifs.[63] While the text of the Song of Songs overflows with marital imagery, Gregory is clear that we are to understand this marriage as union with God: "What is described there is marriage; but what is understood is the union of the human soul with God".[64] The apophatic character of the training contained in this third Solomonic book will become more apparent as we explore the Song of Song's pedagogy of soul's noetic-erotic grasp. As we shall see, one of the keys to understanding the apophatic education of desire that the Song of Songs works on soul is seen in Gregory's identification of the text of the Song of Song's with the Holy of Holies.

The Song of Songs and the Holy of Holies

Gregory says in Homily One, "let each person go out of himself and out of the material world. Let him ascend into paradise through detachment, having become like God through purity".[65] Having thus identified these transfigured epistemological states that result from the exercises of Proverbs and Ecclesiastes (the movement from material to immaterial in a process of divinization (ὁμοιωθεὶς τῷ θεῷ), Gregory says now "let him enter into the inner sanctuary of the mysteries revealed in this book".[66] This alignment of the Song of Songs with the Holy of Holies provides an important clue as to the type of exercise by which the philosophy contained in the Song of Songs will train soul's desire for God.

What exactly Gregory intends by the Holy of Holies is seen more clearly if we look at a couple of key texts describing it.[67] In the *Life of Moses* Gregory comments on Moses' entry into the darkness where God dwells, Gregory says that Moses "entered the Sanctuary of divine mystagogy. There, having disappeared from sight, he was one with the Invisible".[68] It is important to note the apophatic character of this text. Darkness (γνόφος) is nearly always used by Gregory as a technical term to indicate divine incomprehensibility.[69] Moses' entrance into darkness indicates his entrance into the non-discursive. This is given further emphasis by the oxymoronic tenor of Moses' progression into the Holy of Holies. The Greek text says that Moses penetrates the impenetrable (παραδυεὶς τὸ ἄδυτον). Gregory often uses the oxymoronic and other paradoxical expressions to designate that barrier beyond which discursive reason cannot pass.[70] To enter the Holy of Holies is to enter the darkness of unknowing.

Elsewhere in the the *Life of Moses* we find ourselves once again in the Holy of Holies, and once again Gregory bestows on it a deeply apophatic character. He says, "the truth of being is ungraspable (ἄληπτος) and unapproachable (ἀπρόσιτος) to the multitude; since it resides in the impenetrable (ἄδυτος) and forbidden (ἀπόρρητος) regions of the tent of mystery, we should not concern ourselves with the knowledge of realities that transcends our understanding".[71] Again we see the apophatic terminology used to decribe the Holy of Holies: to the grasp of comprehension God is out of reach, remaining hidden in the dark sanctuary. Lest we think that Gregory has in mind a sanctuary made by human hands he says boldly in *Homily Three on the Lord's Prayer* that the real Holy of Holies is "the secret chamber of the heart".[72] The human depths are the hidden dwelling where God is encountered beyond the grasp of comprehension. But these apophatic depths are also the depths of the Song of Songs.

Early on in the *Homilies on the Song of Songs* Gregory identifies the Song of Songs with the Holy of Holies. "Now let us enter the Holy of Holies that is the Song of Songs".[73] After commenting on the significance of the title of the Song of Songs,[74] Gregory says "those who are led into this book's sanctuaries of mystery are no longer human but have been transformed in nature into something more divine by the Lord's teaching".[75] In Homily Three Gregory says the text of the Song of Songs on which he is about to comment is "a participation in divinity itself".[76]

For Gregory of Nyssa, then, the Song of Songs, rich with passionate images as it is, is at the same time the innermost sanctuary, the Holy of Holies, the apophatic space[77] where God is encountered in the darkness of unknowing, beyond the grasp of images and concepts. It is precisely this coincidence of opposites in the Song of Songs (image and imagelessness, passion and dispassion) that characterizes the training of desire that is the specialty of this third Solomonic book.

While clearly Gregory can speak of the equivalence of the Song of Songs and the Holy of Holies, he also speaks of the Song of Songs as the means by which the soul is brought into the inner sanctuary. After the soul has undergone the training of Proverbs and Ecclesiastes, "Solomon [Christ] initiates the soul into the divine sanctuary by means of the Song of Songs".[78] Unlike the pedagogy found in either Proverbs or Ecclesiastes, the Song of Songs wants to lead the soul into the apophatic space of the inner sanctuary, the hidden chamber of the heart, where the Beloved is encountered in the embracing darkness; while eluding every grasp of concept and image, the Beloved is found by the grasp of faith.[79] How then does the Song go about this? What sort of training is contained in the philosophy of the Song of Songs? The fact that Gregory likens the Song of Songs to the Holy of Holies, and even more so by stating that the Song of Song initiates one into the Holy of Holies, suggests that the process by which one enters the apophatic space of the Holy of Holies is the same as that by which one enters the Song of Songs.[80] If the soul is going to be trained by the philosophy contained in the Song of Songs, then, it must ultimately be taught to abandon noetic-erotic control in order to enter the hidden sanctuary, the apophatic space that is the Song of Songs and commune there with the Beloved. This is the function of the intensely evocative images of the Song which attempt to excite and ultimately transform "passion into dispassion".[81]

Apophatic Training in the Song of Songs

The tantalizing images of the Word's previous Solomonic exercises have focused on training the human person to fall in love with divine Beauty. Gregory says quite movingly: "Because Wisdom is speaking, *love* (ἀγάπησον) with all your heart and with all your strength (Dt. 6:5), as much as you can. *Desire* (ἐπιθύμησον) as much as possible. And to these words I boldly add, *'fall in love'* (ἐράσθητι); because this passion (πάθος) for the incorporeal is without reproach and dispassionate (ἀπαθές), as Wisdom says in Proverbs when she enjoins on us to fall in love with divine Beauty".[82] It is important to note what is happening to desire—whether ἀγάπη, ἐπιθυμία, ἔρως, or πάθος[83]—in this text. Far from being eradicated, it is being transfigured by its education and brought to the threshold of the transcendent. While capable of being attracted and attached to material things, the same desire is also capable of being attracted to God.[84] The sense that desire is being brought to the threshold of the transcendent is rendered, however enigmatically, by the apophatic arrangement which concludes the paragraph: desire is led to a state of dispassionate passion. Such paradoxes are typical of Gregory. They constitute the threshold of the apophatic and indicate the border beyond which the noetic-erotic grasp does not pass, implying an ascent to union beyond all image and concept.[85] While this apophatic hue apparently characterizes the end of early Solomonic education of desire it is clearly the primary focus of the Song of Songs.

Gregory says that the Song of Songs "philosophizes through ineffable (ἀπορρήτων) mysteries".[86] That is to say, it exercises the soul by means of the

unutterable; the apophatic character of this pedagogical strategy, as well as
the allusion to the Holy of Holies, indicates how the Song of Songs will lead
the soul to union.[87] Obviously the Song of Songs, of all of the Solomonic
books, is going to use powerfully evocative images to attract and inflame
desire.[88] But it must be kept in mind that the Song of Songs is attempting to
initiate the soul into the apophatic space of the Holy of Holies; Gregory sees
the Song of Songs using powerfully erotic images to bring one to the imageless space of the Holy of Holies, where union with God beyond all image
and concept takes place.

Paradox is rather inevitable and suggested by the structure of the Holy of
Holies itself. At the opening of Homily Two Gregory describes the Holy of
Holies as the "sacred Tent of Witness" and reflects on its description, noting
the contrast between its exterior and interior. The exterior consists of cur-
tains made from linen and goatskins. The interior, by contrast is resplendent
with gold, silver, and precious stones; there is the Ark, the Mercy-Seat,
censer and altar; covering the entrances are veils of blue, purple, flaxen and
scarlet, woven together skillfully with exquisite gold thread, making it shine
like a rainbow (cf. Ex. 26).[89] Immediately he likens this to the Song of Songs,
the true Tent of Witness and "guide in everything concerning philosophy
and the knowledge of God".[90]

The exterior of the Song of Songs is the erotic words and expressions that
arouse desire through descriptions of beautiful things, even exposed bodily
members. The interior of the Song of Songs: a Person of abundant light, full
of mysteries,[91] that is to say, the Beloved, God the Word. What is even more
telling is that when Gregory designates the obstacle to entering the Song of
Songs to commune with God, he shifts from the metaphor of desire to that
of epistemology: thoughts are the obstacle to entering the inner sanctuary
of the Song of Songs.[92] But this should come as no surprise. In Gregory's
well-known ascents to apophatic union, thoughts present the final obstacle
to union and must be abandoned.[93] In order for the human to enter the
Song of Songs, the darkness of the inner sanctuary, one must abandon all
thought.

The pedagogical strategy of the philosophy contained in the Song of
Songs, then, should now be rather more obvious. The outer garments of the
Song, its powerfully evocative images containing the power of the Word,
serve to attract desire which has been inflamed by the Holy Spirit and
trained by the Word through Proverbs and Ecclesiastes, drawing, educating
the noetic-erotic soul yet further to long for what is imageless, beyond the
grasp of comprehension. This "transforms passion (πάθος) into dispassion
(ἀπάθειαν), so that when every corporeal affection has been quenched, our
mind might boil with desire (ἐρωτικῶς) in the Spirit alone and be warmed
by that fire which the Lord came to cast upon the earth".[94] Let us examine
some of the apophatic spaces which reveal this pedagogy of paradox in
operation.

The Inner Sanctuary of Paradise

The Song of Songs itself is a sort of paradox. An image of the imageless, the erotic image of the noetic imageless, the Beloved is the ever present, ever elusive centre of the Song of Songs.[95] Commenting on Song 1:4: "The king has brought me into his chamber", Gregory depicts the soul/bride searching for the Beloved in an apophatic space. She has seen the Beloved's lips and breasts and communed with the Beloved by placing her mouth on his, as he transforms her mouth into a fountain welling forth words of eternal life[96] and now "she has passed with her mind to the inner part of the mysteries and cries out that her passage has only brought her to the vestibule of goodness".[97] Through the purification of the Spirit "she searches the depths of God within the inner sanctuary of paradise and, as the great Paul said, sees things unseen and hears words unspoken".[98]

The way in which the apophatic works on the noetic-erotic grasp typifies the Song of Song's pedagogy. The breasts and lips of the Beloved have attracted the bride/soul,[99] the Spirit has purified her. She enters the innermost sanctuary with her mind and immediately is in a situation of paradox. She is in the sanctuary but seems to think she is in the vestibule.[100] This discursive dislocation brought on by the encounter with the Beloved, ever beyond the grasp of concepts, leaves the bride speaking in Pauline oxymorons, the linguistic signpost of the apophatic: she sees the unseen, hears the inaudible. The bride is in the epistemological darkness of the sanctuary. Through the pedagogy of the Song of Songs, the soul's noetic-erotic grasp has relaxed into open palms of communion.

Interior as this is to the bride, the experience has an ecclesial dimension which Gregory brings out as he comments on Song 1:4: "Let us rejoice and be glad in you." The bride's apophatic experience has caused her maiden companions to rejoice and love her breasts too: "Because you love the Word's breasts more than wine, we shall love and imitate you and love your breasts more than the wine humans make, through which you feed those who are infants in Christ."[101] Through the bride's apophatic union with the Beloved, her breasts take on the character of his breasts; she becomes a source of nourishment, stirring in others the attraction to God which the Word's beauty attracted and the Spirit inflamed in her. This seems to be a characteristic of Gregorian apophaticism, which I have termed "*logophasis*": in the context of apophatic union, the deeds and discourse of the bride take on the attracting, transforming power of the Word and become a vehicle of the Word's incarnational dynamic.[102]

The Darkness of the Wedding Chamber

The faculty of desire (ἡ ἐπιθυμητικὴ δύναμις) is placed in the soul to create a longing for God.[103] The Song of Songs uses erotic images to excite this desire and train it to long for union with God who is beyond the grasp of all image and concept. One such evocative image is the marriage bed, itself a symbol of union.[104] The bride's escorts describe Solomon's bed in Homily Six in order to excite in the bride a desire for union.[105] Indeed the bride has already known union, as we have just seen in Homily One, and she has attained considerable perfection.[106] But this same bed is also surrounded by darkness,[107] and in this darkness she feels she has not even come near perfection. Embraced by this "divine night" she now begins to seek the Beloved "hidden in the darkness" and cries out, "then did I desire my Beloved even though he escapes the grasp of thought".[108] But she continues to seek him. Only when she realizes that he cannot be grasped by thought, that indeed this poses an obstacle,[109] does she realize that the Beloved is known only in unknowing.[110] Abandoning everything she has comprehended, she finds her Beloved, not by the grasp of comprehension but by the ungrasping grasp of faith.[111]

In this moving account of the bride's search for the Beloved we see the Song of Song's pedagogical strategy at work. The erotic image of the marriage bed (union with the Word) is placed before the bride. This stirs her desire to seek the Beloved (the work of the Spirit, though admittedly more muted here). Immediately the context shifts to the apophatic, signalled by stock Gregorian apophatic markers such as darkness and various oxymoronic expressions: she is in a state of perfection yet at the very beginning of her journey; she knows by unknowing; she grasps by the grasp of faith what by definition can never be grasped. Moreover, we see desire, attracted and excited (again the interplay of Word and Spirit), move not only into the apophatic darkness, but beyond thoughts seemingly right to union by faith with the Beloved. Indeed the ungrasping grasp of union by faith has transfigured the noetic-erotic grasp to an open palm of exhilarated receptivity. Lastly, we see once again this apophatic education of desire overflow into the logophatic: The bride turns and speaks to the daughters of Jerusalem. This speech has the same effect on them that the Word had on her. Therefore, they too "ascend to an equal measure of love so that the Bridegroom's will might be fulfilled in them".[112]

Wounded By Love

Certainly one of the more intriguing exercises contained in the Song of Songs features Gregory's highly provocative triptych of the wound of love in Homilies Four, Twelve and Thirteen.[113] In the most extended treatment of this theme, Homily Four features the arrow as an explicitly Trinitarian image. The archer is love (ἀγάπη), later identified as God, and the arrow itself is the only begotten Son. The tip of the arrow (faith) is triple-pointed, dipped and moistened in the Spirit.[114] While the Word's typical attraction of the bride and the Spirit's inflaming of her desire play less a role, it is nevertheless present in this triptych of wounding love. The wounds created by the arrow are beautiful and desireable and inflame yet more vehement desire.[115]

The bride cries out, "I am wounded by love", and is immediately immersed in an apophatic context indicated by oxymoronic expressions and images of union. She continues her exclamation, boasting in oxymorons, "O beautiful wound and sweet blow by which life, penetrates within! The arrow's penetration opens up, as it were, a door and entrance for love. As soon as the bride receives the arrow of love, the imagery shifts from archery to nuptial delight".[116] In Homily Twelve it is a "divine rod or Spirit" that delivers the wound. Like Paul rejoicing in his wounds, the bride likewise expresses this oxymoronically as a beautiful wound, a boastful wound, a healing blow.[117] The oxymorons suggest the apophatic boundary beyond which discursive reason does not pass and prepare her for union by exercising desire and delight in this boastful wound.

This description of union is extraordinary indeed, as the bride is taken into the dynamism of the Trinity. The bride marvels at the sight of the divine arrow within herself, but no sooner does she notice than she amazingly becomes the arrow which has penetrated her. Conflating the images of Archer and Bridegroom, Gregory depicts the bride as both embraced by the Beloved and held by the Archer as an arrow in the bow, ready to be shot forth.[118] In a striking coincidence of opposites that designates the apophatic space we are in, Gregory has the bride proclaim: " 'His right hand receives me and draws me back, easing my journey upward where I am directed without being separated from the archer. Simultaneously I am carried away by this act of shooting and am at rest in the hands of the bowman'".[119]

In an understated logophatic gesture, the bride then addresses the daughters of Jerusalem. The logophatic effect is not as well developed here as in Homily Four, but in Homily Thirteen it is more clearly evident. "Inflamed with love, the bride reveals the shaft of love placed deeply in her heart, for this signifies communion (κοινωνία) with God".[120] This manifestation effects profoundly the bride's companions. They begin to reflect on her various ascents throughout the *Homilies on the Song of Songs* with the result that they begin to desire the Beloved: " 'Tell us of your Beloved and of his nature. Give us, you who are filled with loveliness, "beautiful among women", a means to recognize him. Indicate to us the one whom you seek, and teach us by what signs this unseen lover can be found, that we may know him by the shaft of love which wounded your heart and intensified your desire for him through sweet pain'."[121] The bride's desire, attracted by the Word and inflamed by the Spirit, has awakened the same desire for the Beloved in the daughters of Jerusalem.

Conclusion

To interpret the Song of Songs is to be drawn in to the Holy of Holies. The imageless silence of the sanctuary is the innermost reality of the sacred text whose sole purpose is to lead soul to union. We have seen that Gregory sees in this a rather explicit pedagogy for this very purpose. With desire strengthened, purified, inflamed, and educated by the exercises of the philosophy contained in Proverbs and Ecclesiastes, the soul is ready for Solomon's supreme tutelage, the Song of Songs. Filled with erotic images of passionate love, the Song of Songs educates the soul to long for and commune with the divine beauty of the Bridegroom. But to do this, the soul must learn something not taught by Proverbs or Ecclesiastes. Noetic-erotic grasping poses a problem and must be taught to abandon control; for in the inner sanctuary of divine presence, there is no object for desire or concept to grasp. She must learn to enter, desire inflamed, with open palms of unknowing. To facilitate this the philosophy contained in the Song of Songs exercises the soul with paradox and oxymoron: luminous dark; sober inebriation; boastful wound; sweet pain; knowing by unknowing; ungrasping grasp; at the summit of perfection she is yet a beginner; she is at once in the inner sanctuary and the outer vestibule; she is both wounded by the arrow of love and becomes a wounding arrow of love; at movement and at rest. Paradox unclenches noetic-erotic fists of comprehension: "having forsaken every manner of comprehension, I found my beloved by faith".[122]

For Gregory of Nyssa, Solomon's tutelage is from first to last Trinitarian. The erotic Beauty of the Word in Scripture attracts desire that is excited and inflamed by the Spirit. The divine Archer shoots the Spirit-moistened arrow of the Son. Penetrated by this arrow, she is ever moving repose and becomes a vehicle of presence for all to see. At rest in the Bridegroom's embrace, she is at the same time shot forth in mission for all the daughters of Jerusalem.

NOTES

1 M. Hart, "Reconciliation of Body and Soul: Gregory of Nyssa's Deeper Theology of Marriage", *Theological Studies* 51 (1990), pp. 450–478; see also his "Gregory of Nyssa's Ironic Praise of the Celibate Life", *Heythrop Journal* 32 (1992), pp. 1–19.
2 J. Behr, "The Rational Animal: A Rereading of Gregory of Nyssa's *De hominis opificio*", *Journal of Early Christian Studies* 7 (1999), pp. 219–247.
3 R. Williams, "Macrina's Deathbed Revisited: Gregory of Nyssa on Mind and Passion", in L. Wickham and C. Bammel (eds), *Christian Faith and Greek Philosophy in Late Antiquity* (Leiden: E. J. Brill, 1993), pp. 227–246.
4 M. Ludlow, *Universal Salvation: Eschatology in the Thought of Gregory of Nyssa and Karl Rahner* (Oxford: Oxford University Press, 2000), especially pp. 56–64.
5 While less closely related to the argument pursued in this essay, the following contributions should not be overlooked: V. Burrus, *Begotten not Made: Conceiving Manhood in Late Antiquity* (Stanford, CA: Stanford University Press, 2000); P. Huybrechts, " 'Traité de la Virginitate' de Grégoire de Nysse: Idéal de vie monastique ou idéal de vie chrétienne", *Nouvelle Revue Théologique* 115 (1993), pp. 227–242; V. E. F. Harrison, "Male and Female in Cappadocian Theology", *Journal of Theological Studies* (NS) 41 (1990), pp. 441–471; T. Shaw, *The Burden of the Flesh: Fasting and Sexuality in Early Christianity* (Minneapolis, MN: Fortress Press, 1998), esp. pp. 92–96; P. Brown. *The Body and Society: Men, Women, and Sexual Renunciation in Early Christianity* (New York, NY: Columbia University Press, 1988), pp. 285–304, on which see the comments of J. Behr, "Shifting Sands: Foucault, Brown and the Framework of Christian Asceticism", *Heythrop Journal* 34 (1993), pp. 1–21; for a concise overview of research on asceticism in recent years see Behr's recent, *Asceticism and Anthropology in Irenaeus and Clement* (Oxford: Oxford University Press, 2000), pp. 5–15.

6   It is important to be aware of a certain lack of consistency in Gregory's vocabulary of desire. A common word like ἐπιθυμία can be used in the negative sense of lust (hence Behr's translation below) but also quite positively in the sense of desire for God. Gregory can even use a word like πάθος, usually quite negative, in a positive sense of having a πάθος for the incorporeal (*In Cant.* I, 23, 10). Similar ambivalence can be seen in Gregory's use of words built on ἔρως. In the *Homilies on the Song of Songs* ἐπιθυμία will figure largely as the focus of the pedagogy. I will translate it as desire. When I believe it is important that the reader know what other items in the vocabulary of desire I am translating, I will supply the Greek term. In his notes to his yet unpublished translation of the *Homilies on the Song of Songs*, R. Norris has speculated on why such usage of terms for desire occur. Intriguingly Norris suggests a possible stimulus from Origen, who, in his *Commentary on the Song of Songs*, discusses "various Greek words that English tends perforce to render by the single term 'love'". Taking this queue I allow "desire" to translate a number of words (ἐπιθυμία, ἔρως, ἔφεσις, πόθος, even at times πάθος); for, as Ludlow will point out what is important about desire is its malleable quality, its capacity to focus on blind impulse or on God. Hence the Solomonic concern to train desire.

7   On the dating of Gregory's works see J. Daniélou, "La chronologie des oeuvres de Grégoire de Nysse", *Studia Patristica* 7 (1966), pp. 159–179; see also G. May, "Die Chronologie des Lebens und der Werke des Gregor von Nyssa" in M. Harl (ed), *Écriture et Culture dans la Pensée de Grégoire de Nysse* (Leiden: E. J. Brill, 1971), pp. 51–67, and the more recent summary of A. Cortesi, *Le "Omelie sul Cantico dei Cantici" di Gregorio di Nissa: Proposta di un itinerario di vita battesimale*. Studia Ephemeridis Augustinianum 70 (Rome: Institutum Patristicum Augustinianum, 2000), pp. 9–22.

8   M. Hart, "Reconciliation of Body and Soul", p. 451.

9   Ibid.

10   Ibid., p. 463.

11   Following the convention of *The Philokalia*, 4 vols, trans. G. Palmer, P. Sherrard, K. Ware (London: Faber and Faber, 1979–), I will translate ἀπάθεια as "dispassion".

12   J. Behr, "The Rational Animal", p. 232.

13   Ibid.

14   On which see below.

15   *De hominis opificio*, in J. P. Migne (ed) *Patrologia Graeca* (Paris, 1857–1866), 44, 193b, cited in Behr, "The Rational Animal", p. 246.

16   J. Behr, "The Rational Animal", p. 246.

17   C. Stead, "The Concept of the Mind and the Concept of God in the Christian Fathers", in B. Hebblethwaite and S. Sunderland (eds), *The Philosophical Frontiers of Christian Theology* (Cambridge: Cambridge University Press, 1982), pp. 39–54.

18   C. Stead, "The Concept of the Mind and the Concept of God in the Christian Fathers", p. 48.

19   R. Williams, "Macrina's Deathbed Revisted", p. 229.

20   Ibid., p. 236.

21   Ibid., p. 235.

22   M. Ludlow, *Universal Salvation*, p. 57.

23   Ibid., p. 64.

24   Ibid., p. 63.

25   Ibid., p. 58.

26   R. Williams, "Macrina's Deathbed Revisited", p. 235.

27   For a concise overview of this question, especially its Platonic and Stoic inflections, see J. Dillon, "Rejecting the Body, Refining the Body: Some Remarks on the Development of Platonist Asceticism" in V. Wimbush and R. Valantasis (eds), *Asceticism* (Oxford: Oxford University Press, 1995), pp. 80–87. See also K. Ware, " 'My Helper and my Enemy': the Body in Greek Christianity", in S. Coakley (ed), *Religion and the Body* (Cambridge: Cambridge University Press, 1997), pp. 90–110.

28   See *De vita Moysis*, II, 157, 12. All references to this work are to book, chapter and line of the critical edition prepared and introduced by J. Daniélou, *La Vie de Moïse*, Sources Chrétiennes (hereafter SC) 1bis (Paris: Cerf, 1987).

29   See Gregory of Nyssa, *Commentarius in Canticum canticorum* (hereafter *In Cant.*), VI,182, 18–183, 8. All references to this work are to the critical edition prepared and introduced

by H. Langerbeck in W. Jaeger (gen. ed), Gregorii Nysseni Opera (hereafter GNO) vol. VI (Leiden: Brill, 1986). References are first to the homily in Roman numerals, followed by the page and line of the critical edition. For English translation I have relied on *Commentary on the Song of Songs*, C. McCambley, trans., The Archbishop Iakovos Library of Historical Sources 12 (Brookline, MA: Hellenic College Press, 1987). I have also profited by reading the unpublished translation of The Rev. Prof. Richard Norris.

30 Hart, Behr and Williams have based their arguments on *De virginitate, De anima et resurrectione*, and *De hominis opificio*. There are other examples, drawn from later works in Gregory's career that can be read in support of their claims. See for example *Oratio catechetica* VI, GNO III/iv, 22,11 where humanity is described as a mixture or blending (μιγμα) of the intelligible and the sensible. See also Gregory's use of such terms as αἴσθησις, ὁρμή, and ἐπιθυμία in *De vita Moysis* II, 122; 157, 10–11. Gregory's interesting use of the term πολυπραγμοσύνη also supports the line of argument in question. It is used in a pejorative sense to describe the meddlesomeness of the mind at *Contra Eunomium*, GNO II, 253, 28 and at *In Cant*. XI, 339, 17. But the same term can be used in a quite positive sense to describe the dynamic quality of the mind that allows it to penetrate into the incomprehensible where God is seen; see *De vita Moysis*, II, 163, 3–5 and *In Cant*. VI, 182, 18.

31 *In Cant*. I, 27, 11–12: μετενεγκοῦσαν εἰς ἀπάθειαν τὸ πάθος, … Translation altered.

32 Origen, *Commentarius in Canticum canticorum*, Prol. 2, 39, SC 375. English translation in R. Lawson (trans.), *The Song of Songs Commentary and Homilies*. Ancient Christian Writers 26 (New York: Newman Press, 1957), p. 36.

33 Obviously, however, Origen does not deny that the Fall has affected desire.

34 Origen specifies in the course of the Prologue the specific pedagogical function of each of these books.

35 Solomon is later identified as "a type of Christ" at Prol. 4, 17.

36 Origen, *Commentarius in Canticum canticorum*, Prol. 3, 7; translation altered.

37 In his own prologue to his *Homilies on the Song of Songs*, Gregory acknowledges a clear debt to Origen. See R. Heine, "Gregory of Nyssa's Apology for Allegory", *Vigiliae Christianae* 38 (1984), pp. 360–370. This does not, however, mean that Gregory follows Origen in all matters; for a concise discussion of convergences and divergences in Origen and Gregory see F. Dünzl, "Die Canticum-Exegese des Gregor von Nyssa und des Origenes im Vergleich", *Jahrbuch für Antike und Christentum* 36 (1993), pp. 94–109; A. Meredith, "Origen's *De Principiis* and Gregory of Nyssa's *Oratio Catechetica*", *Heythrop Journal* 36 (1995), pp. 1–14; idem *The Cappadocians* (London: Geoffrey Chapman, 1995), pp. 54–62; R. Placida, "La presenza di Origene nelle Omelie sul Cantico dei Cantici di Gregorio di Nissa", *Vetera Christianorum* 34 (1997), pp. 33–49.

38 On the question of literary genre see the discussion of F. Dünzl, *Braut und Braütigam: Die Auslegung des Canticum durch Gregor von Nyssa* (Tübingen: J. C. B. Mohr, 1993), pp. 7–16, especially p. 10.

39 On the characteristic functions of the prologue in a commentary in the patristic period see A. Di Berardino and B. Studer, *History of Theology: The Patristic Period*, M. O'Connell, trans. (Collegeville, MN: The Liturgical Press 1997), pp. 301–302.

40 By "prologue" I obviously do not intend the prefatory letter addressed to Olympias and containing his defense of allegory.

41 A. DiBerardino and B. Studer, *A History of Theology: The Patristic Period*, pp. 301–302.

42 P. Hadot, *Philosophy as a Way of Life*, trans. M. Chase, (Oxford: Blackwell, 1985), especially pp. 126–144; idem, *Qu'est-ce que la philosophie antique?* (Paris: Gallimard, 1995), especially pp. 355–378 and 381–387; I. Hadot, "The Spiritual Guide", in A. Armstrong (ed), *Classical Mediterranean Spirituality* (New York, NY: Crossroad, 1986), pp. 436–459, especially pp. 450–455.

43 A. Di Berardino and B. Studer, *History of Theology: The Patristic Period*, p. 4; C. Desalvo, *L' "oltre" nel presente: La filosofia dell' uomo di Gregorio di Nissa* (Milan: Centro di Ricerche di Metafisica, 1996), pp. 137–142. See also the classic study of A. Malingrey, *Philosophia. Etude d'un group de mots dans la littérature grecque des Présocratiques au IVe siècle après J. C.* (Paris, 1961).

44 See, for example, *In Cant*. I, 17, 11 and 22, 8.

45 Following Origen, Solomon is Christ; see *In Cant*. I, 17, 1–3.

46 Ibid., 18, 7–10.

47 Ibid., 22, 9: … εἰς τὴν τῶν ἀρετῶν ἐπιθυμίαν.

48 Ibid., 19, 17–20, 9.
49 Ibid., 23, 8–9: ἐπιθύμησον ὅσον χωρεῖς. προστίθημι δὲ θαρρῶν τοῖς ῥήμασι τούτοις καὶ τὸ ἐράσθητι.
50 Ibid., 23, 9–12; translation my own.
51 Ibid., 22, 7–9.
52 Ibid., 22, 13–15. The description of the philosophical exercise contained in Ecclesiastes is far briefer than that described in Proverbs. It has been suggested by Verna Harrison that this is due possibly to the fact that Gregory has already a series of homilies on Ecclesiastes and no such work devoted to Proverbs. See V. E. F. Harrison, "A Gender Reversal in Gregory of Nyssa's *First Homily on the Song of Songs*", *Studia Patristica* 27 (1993), pp. 34–38 at p. 36.
53 *In Cant.* I, 19, 11; 21, 16; 22, 14.
54 Obviously Gregory is much inspired by Origen's understanding of how these three Solomonic books exercise the soul; however, Gregory seems less attached to a strict division between beginner, proficient and perfect and, more notably, emphasizes divine union.
55 *In Cant.* I, 17, 2–3.
56 Ibid., 17, 7–12.
57 M. Canévet, *Grégoire de Nysse et l'herméneutique biblique: Étude des rapports entre le langage et la connaissance de Dieu* (Paris: Études Augustiniennes, 1983), p. 326.
58 *In Cant.* I, 14, 1ff.: "Those of you who, according to the advice of St. Paul, have stripped off the old man … and have wrapped yourselves … in the bright garments of the Lord; … you who have been transformed with him into a state free from passion and more divine, listen to the mysteries of the Song of Songs. Enter the inner chamber of the chaste bridegroom and clothe yourselves with the white garments of pure chaste thoughts." On the question of the audience to whom Gregory delivers the homilies see F. Dünzl, *Braut und Bräutigam*, pp. 26–30; see also A. Cortesi, *Le "Omelie sul Cantico dei Cantici" di Gregorio di Nissa: Proposta di un itinerario di vita battesimale.* Studia Ephemeridis Augustinianum 70 (Rome: Institutum Patristicum Augustinianum, 2000).
59 M. Canévet, "Exégèse et théologie dans les traités spirituels de Grégoire de Nysse", in Marguerite Harl (ed), *Ecriture et culture philosophique dans la pensée de Grégoire de Nysse* (Leiden: E. J. Brill, 1971), pp. 146–147. Canévet makes reference to J. Daniélou's article, "Chrismation prébaptismale et divinité de l'Esprit chez Grégoire de Nysse", *Recherches des Science Religieuses* 56 (1968), pp. 177–198, where he argues that baptism also suggests the pre-baptismal annointing, heavily suggestive of the Holy Spirit.
60 The remarks of M. Canévet regarding the Trinitarian theology in Gregory's exegetical works are worthy of note. Answering why it is that Gregory's exegetical works often do not make explicit reference to the divine persons he says: "Nous croyons pouvoir expliquer ce fait, au premier abord surprenant, par la théologie grégorienne elle-même que est préoccupée d'affirmer l'identité d'action des trois Personnes, preuve de leur identité de nature, plus que de définir les relations intra-trinitaires. En dehors des discussions dogmatiques, Grégoire parle plus volontiers du 'divin', de 'Dieu', de la 'nature divine', lorsque l'économie du salut est en cause;…" (*Grégoire de Nysse et l'herméneutique biblique*, p. 248.)
61 On the dating of the *Homilies on the Song of Songs*, see J. Cahill, "The Date and Setting of Gregroy of Nyssa's 'Commentary on the Song of Songs'", *Journal of Theological Studies*, NS 32 (1981), pp. 447–460. Cf. the position of F. Dünzl, "Gregor von Nyssa's *Homilien zum Canticum* auf dem Hintergrund seiner *Vita Moysis*", *Vigiliae Christianae* 44 (1990), pp. 371–381.
62 *In Cant.* I, 15, 13–15: διὰ γὰρ τῶν ἐνταῦθα γεγραμμένων νυμφοστολεῖται τρόπον τινὰ ἡ ψυχὴ πρὸς τὴν ἀσώματόν τε καὶ πνευματικήν καὶ ἀμόλυντον τοῦ θεοῦ συζυγίαν. Translation altered.
63 See F. Vinel in her translation of Gregory's *Homelies sur l'Ecclesiaste*, SC 416 (Paris: Cerf, 1996), p. 388, n. 2; for a general discusssion of apophatic language in the Cappadocians see J. Pelikan, *Christianity and Classical Culture: The Metamorphosis of Natural Theology in the Christian Encounter with Hellenism* (New Haven, CT: Yale University Press, 1993), pp. 40–56.
64 Ibid., 22, 18–23, 1: ἐν οἷς τὸ μὲν ὑπογραφόμενον ἐπιθαλάμιός τίς ἐστι διασκευή, τὸ δὲ νοούμενον τῆς ἀνθρωπίνης ψυχῆς ἡ πρὸς τὸ θεῖόν ἐστιν ἀνάκρασις.
65 Ibid., 25, 6–9.
66 Ibid., 25, 9–10.
67 There is some discussion of whether the composition of the *Life of Moses* precedes or follows that of the *Homilies on the Song of Songs*. Both works come from the end of his career.

68   *De vita Moysis*, I, 46, 4–5.
69   M. Simonetti, ed and trans., *Vita di Mosè*, Scrittori Greci e Latini (Milan: Mondadori, 1984), pp. 269–270.
70   See for example *In Cant*. V, 156, 18; see also J. Daniélou, *Platonisme et théologie mystique: Essai sur la doctrine spirituelle de Saint Grégoire de Nysse* (Paris: Aubier, 2nd ed., 1953), pp. 274ff.; J. Williams, *Denying Divinity: Apophasis in the Patristic Christian and Soto Zen Buddhist Traditions* (Oxford: Oxford University Press, 2000), pp. 202–203 et passim.
71   *De vita Moysis*, II, 188, 4–8.
72   *De orat. dom.* III, GNO VII, ii, 31–32f. For provocative resonances in Plotinus see *Enn.* V, 1, 6 and VI, 9, 11.
73   *In Cant*. I, 26, 11–12; translation altered. Midrash on the Song of Songs I. 1 and 11 ascribed to Rabbi Akiba: "all the Writings are holy and this is the holy of holies". My thanks to Rev. Prof. Richard Norris for this citation. See U. Neri, *Il Cantico dei Cantici: Targum e antiche interpretazioni ebraiche* (Rome, 1976).
74   A standard way for beginning a commentary; see A. DiBerardino and B. Studer, *History of Theology*, pp. 301–302.
75   *In Cant*. I, 29, 13–16; translation altered.
76   *In Cant*. III, 71, 5–6.
77   See G. Ward, "Allegoria: Reading as a Spiritual Exercise", *Modern Theology* 15 (1999), pp. 271–295 at pp. 286–287.
78   *In Cant*. I, 22, 16–17.
79   See *In Cant*. VI, 183, 9.
80   See R. Norris, "The Soul Takes Flight: Gregory of Nyssa and the Song of Songs", *Anglican Theological Review* 80 (1998), pp. 517–532 at 526; see also C. MacLeod, "Allegory and Mysticism in Origen and Gregory of Nyssa", *Journal of Theological Studies* n.s. 22 (1971), pp. 362–379.
81   *In Cant*. I, 27, 11–12; translation altered.
82   Ibid., 23, 6–12. Emphasis added; translation my own.
83   The inspiration of Origen's discussion of the overlapping semantic fields of these terms should not go without saying. See Origen's discussion in the Prologue to his *Commentarius in Canticum canticorum*, Prol. 2. On the vocabulary of love see the discussion of C. Osborne, *Eros Unveiled: Plato and the God of Love* (Oxford: Oxford University Press, 1994), pp. 24–85 and pp. 164–184.
84   This reading of Gregory in the *Homilies on the Song of Songs* is consistent with Behr's reading of Gregory's *De opificio hominis*; see J. Behr, "The Rational Animal", pp. 232–233.
85   See J. Daniélou, *Platonisme et théologie mystique*, pp. 274–284; M. Canévet claims that Gregory's paradoxes ultimately are grounded in the person of Christ, an insight which harmonizes well with our observation that the Word is the pedagogue in the Song of Songs; see M. Canévet, *Grégoire de Nysse et l'herméneutique biblique*, p. 342.
86   *In Cant*. I, 23, 14.
87   Gregory uses ἀπορρήτων also when referring to the inner regions of the mind; see *De vita Moysis* II, 188, 10. On the apophatic character of this term in Gregory see J. Daniélou, *Platonisme et théologie mystique*, pp. 182–189.
88   As indicated above, the Trinitarian dynamic of the pedagogical initiative should not be lost sight of even if Gregory does not always bring it out.
89   *In Cant*. II, 43, 8–44, 7.
90   Ibid., 44, 9–10.
91   Ibid., 44, 16–17. It should not surprise us that Christ is for Gregory the inner reality of the Song of Songs: in *De vita Moysis*, II, 174, Christ is identified as the inner reality of the Tent. See R. Norris, "The Soul Takes Flight: Gregory of Nyssa and the Song of Songs", p. 524.
92   Ibid., 45, 4–11.
93   See, for example, Abraham in *Contra Eunomium*, GNO I, 252, 1–253, 28, and the bride in *In Cant*. VI, 182, 2–183, 15.
94   *In Cant*. I, 27, 11–15; translation altered. Again note the Trinitarian dimension; see Canévet's observation on the Trinity in *Grégoire de Nysse et l'herméneutique biblique*, p. 248.
95   See R. Norris, "The Soul Takes Flight: Gregory of Nyssa and the Song of Songs", p. 524.
96   See *In Cant*. I, 32.
97   *In Cant*. I, 40, 5–8; translation altered.

98 Ibid., 40, 9–12.

99 Gregory is commenting on Song of Songs 1, 2–4: "Let him kiss me with the kisses of his mouth, for your breasts are better than wine. And the scent of your ointments is better than all spices. Your name is ointment poured forth. Therefore have the young maidens loved you. They have drawn you. We will run after you toward the scent of your ointments. The king has brought me into his chamber. Let us rejoice and be glad in you. Let us love your breasts more than wine. Righteousness has loved you".

100 Obviously Gregory's doctrine of *epektasis* is in the background here; the end of one ascent is the beginning of another.

101 *In Cant.* I, 41, 1–4; translation altered.

102 In any number of apophatic encounters in the *Homilies on the Song of Songs*, Gregory emphasizes, sometimes quite subtly, how the person who experiences union (Paul, Thekla, the Beloved Disciple, the bride) is transformed and becomes a vehicle of the Word, allowing the Word itself to speak through the words and actions of the person in question; hence, the term *"logo-phasis"*, the Word speaking. In this instance, the bride at the zenith of an apophatic ascent, in which she has let go of concepts, images, and all manner of knowing, exhibits, paradoxically, transformed discourse. This transformation is not seen so much in what she has to say, but in the *effects* her speech has on those around her, e.g., the daughters of Jerusalem. They too are stirred and attracted to the Bridegroom. Moreover, this transformation is not limited to discourse. The power of the Word speaking is also revealed in the deeds of the Beloved Disciple or Thekla. *Logophasis*, then, pertains to the transformed and transforming deeds and discourse that result from apophatic union. For more on this theme, see M. Laird, "Apophasis and Logophasis in Gregory of Nyssa", *Studia Patristica* 37 (2001), pp. 126–132.

103 *In Cant.* IV, 119, 5–6.

104 In a rather more ecclesially oriented portion of Homily IV, "bed" is identified with divine union; see *In Cant.* IV, 108, 11 and 109, 1.

105 *In Cant.* VI, 190, 2–3. Gregory has told us that we are to understand marriage as signifying union (*In Cant.* I, 22, 19–23, 1).

106 A summary of her impressive ascents can be found at *In Cant.* VI, 175, 16–179, 20.

107 Just earlier at *In Cant.* VI, 181. Gregory is commenting on Song of Songs 3, 1: "By night on my bed I sought him whom my soul loves. I sought him, but did not find him. I called him but heard him not".

108 *In Cant.* VI 181, 14–16.

109 Cf. *De vita Moysis* II, 165, 6–9: any concept that attempts to attain or define the divine "becomes and idol of God and does not make him known".

110 *In Cant.* VI, 183, 2–3: τὸ ἐν μόνῳ τῷ μὴ καταλαμβάνεσθαι τί ἐστιν ὅτι ἔστι γινωσκόμενον, … This coincidence of knowing and unknowing is an apophatic commonplace, formulated as perfect oxymoron by Augustine as "learned ignnorance" (*Epistula* 130, 15, 28).

111 *In Cant.* VI, 183, 7–9. In this context "faith" serves as a faculty of apophatic union. Gregory uses the term grasp, but it is not the grasp of comprehension (hence and ungrasping grasp of faith); see M. Laird, " 'By Faith Alone': A Technical Term in Gregory of Nyssa", *Vigiliae Christianae* 54 (2000), pp. 61–79.

112 *In Cant.* VI, 184, 14–15.

113 Respectively Sg. 2:4, "I am wounded with love"; Sg. 5:7, "They smote me, they wounded me"; Sg. 5:8, "If you should find my Beloved, tell him I am wounded with love".

114 *In Cant.* IV, 127, 10–14; Dünzl, *Braut und Bräutigam*, p. 375, sees in this image an allusion to baptism as well.

115 *In Cant.* XII, 366, 6–7; *In Cant.* XIII, 377, 20 and 380, 4–6.

116 *In Cant.* IV, 128, 2–7.

117 See *In Cant.* XII, 365, 12–366, 9.

118 This blending of images accommodates the shift in imagery in the Song of Songs itself from that of archery to that of marriage: Sg. 2:5b–6, "I am wounded with love. His left hand is under my head, and his right hand shall embrace me".

119 *In Cant.* IV, 129, 12–16.

120 *In Cant.* XIII, 378, 14–17; translation altered.

121 Ibid., 379, 16–380, 6.

122 *In Cant.* VI, 183, 7–8.

6

"PERSON" VERSUS "INDIVIDUAL", AND OTHER MODERN MISREADINGS OF GREGORY OF NYSSA

LUCIAN TURCESCU

Introduction

During the past three decades, Greek Orthodox theologian John Zizioulas (Metropolitan of Pergamon) has been preoccupied with defining a Christian notion of person which would allow for a better integration of an ontology of personhood with ecclesiology. A person, he tells us, should not be understood as an individual, because in our times individualism has acquired some negative connotations: first, individualism leads to isolation of humans from other humans and, second, it leads to isolation of humans from the rest of the creation, and thus to ecological disasters. Instead, a person should be generous, friendly, and open to others. A person should be communitarian and relational. In opposition to this, the "western" view of person, represented according to Zizioulas by such twentieth century writers as Webb, Walgrave, and Strawson,[1] emphasizes too much that a person is an individual and a center of consciousness.

Yet Zizioulas proposes an alternative to what he calls the "western" understanding of person. If one were to use the views of the Cappadocian Fathers —Basil of Caesarea, Gregory of Nyssa, and Gregory of Nazianzus—and of other Greek Orthodox theologians, one would get the relational, communitarian concept of person which is so much more meaningful today. The relational view of person makes more sense in today's secular world, as we seem to be more concerned with staying in touch, with respect for each other, in general with better relating to each other, as well as with globalization and

Lucian Turcescu
Religious Studies Department and Catholic Studies Program, St. Francis Xavier University, Antigonish, Nova Scotia, B2G 2W5, Canada

protecting the environment. But this view makes sense in the Church also, since Christians share or strive to share the same cup and, in so doing, we want to express our communion with both Christ and our fellow Christians. Zizioulas's concept of person is a meaningful and seemingly coherent concept, showing his interest in modern issues and his attempts to use ancient insights to address them.

Zizioulas has attempted to use insights from the Greek Fathers to shape a concept more suitable for his purposes; and let me say that he is not alone in his efforts.[2] The newly minted concept of person rests on an understanding of the Christian Trinity mainly as prototype of persons-in-relation. The proponents of this view argue that their concept of human person has its antecedent in a theological debate over divine persons, quite clearly articulated by a group of fourth-century Greek theologians known as the "Cappadocian Fathers".[3] For their contribution to the clarification of the notion of person, Zizioulas credits the Cappadocian Fathers with having introduced a personalistic revolution in Greek ontology. In his view, "Person is now the ultimate ontological category we can apply to God",[4] and in many of his articles he emphasizes that person as a category is ontologically prior to substance in the Cappadocian Fathers.[5]

In this essay I propose to investigate whether the Greek Fathers' concept of person provides support for Zizioulas's own concept of person. After presenting some of Zizioulas's views on person, I will contrast them with several important instances in Gregory of Nyssa, in order to demonstrate that the answer to the proposed question is "No". The next step will be to suggest some possible modern authors who have influenced Zizioulas's view of person. In doing so, I will demonstrate that although very creative in his own personalistic ontology, when he tries to integrate the Greek patristic tradition with modern concerns about person, Zizioulas ends up using modern insights of person which he then tries to foist on the Cappadocian Fathers.[6]

Presentation of Zizioulas's Views

Here are the three points Zizioulas disavows in what he perceives to be the modern, "western", understanding of person:

First, he says that personhood should not be understood as "a complex of natural, psychological or moral qualities which are in some sense 'possessed' by or 'contained' in the human *individuum*".[7] Then, when talking about the uniqueness of the person in *Being as Communion*, the book that consecrated him, Zizioulas says that the survival of the uniqueness cannot be ensured by any property of the substance or nature.[8] In his later writings, he repeats but also expands a little on earlier statements, thus showing that his views on the subject might have evolved slightly but have not changed dramatically:

> Personhood is not about qualities or capacities of any kind: biological, social or moral. Personhood is about hypostasis, i.e. the claim to *uniqueness*

in the absolute sense of the term, and this cannot be guaranteed by reference to sex or function or role, or even cultivated consciousness of the "self" and its psychological experiences, since all of these can be classified, thus representing qualities shared by more than one being and not point to absolute uniqueness.[9]

To summarize this view, one could say that, since no biological, social or moral property is unique, neither can the sum of these properties be something unique. Since a person is something unique, the sum of the above properties cannot be considered an appropriate definition of personhood. But maybe it is exactly this coming together of properties which are not themselves unique that makes for a unique combination. We will see shortly what Gregory of Nyssa has to say on that issue.

Second, the individual is partial, according to Zizioulas, because it is subject to addition and combination, whereas a person is free from such boundaries of the "self" as individualization, comprehension, combination, definition, description and use.[10] In *Being as Communion* he makes a similar statement, saying that: "The person is so absolute in its uniqueness that it does not permit itself to be regarded as an arithmetical concept, to be set alongside other beings, to be combined with other objects, or to be used as a means, even for the most sacred goal. The goal is the person itself; personhood is the total fulfillment of being."[11] What probably bothers Zizioulas here is that the individual, by being counted, can be part of statistics, whereas a person is so unique in his view that any attempt to make it part of statistics is to be shunned as a hubris against the deepest and most sacred aspects of being itself.

Third, Zizioulas contends that, based on a cross-fertilization between Boethian and Augustinian anthropologies, western philosophy and culture have come up with an understanding of a person as an individual and a personality, that is, "a unit endowed with intellectual, psychological and moral qualities centred on the axis of consciousness".[12] Zizioulas concludes one of his earliest articles on person by writing: "[I]ndividualisation is precisely the fact that accounts for the impossibility of real communion, because it implies distance and hence division instead of difference."[13] A person, however, wants "to exist as a concrete, unique and unrepeatable entity".[14] But Zizioulas himself perceives a certain weakness in his argument, as the word "entity" and the search for uniqueness, in fact, lead back to individual, the exact same notion from which he wants to liberate the concept of person. In commenting on the person's tendency to regard itself as its own goal, he writes: "For applied to man [this tendency] leads to the denial of others, to egocentrism, to the total destruction of social life ... [Therefore,] a relativisation appears to be indispensable if chaos is to be avoided. Thus, uniqueness is relativised in social life, and man becomes ... a useful 'object', a 'combination', a persona."[15]

Does Zizioulas Understand Correctly Gregory of Nyssa's Concept of Person?

In this section I propose to look at how Gregory of Nyssa understands some of the notions Zizioulas rejects when speaking of person. In doing so, I will attempt to demonstrate that, despite his claims that he relies on the Cappadocian and other Greek theologians when elaborating his own concept of person, Zizioulas misrepresents Cappadocian theology. The topics to be dealt with here are the ones just presented, namely the person as a complex of qualities possessed by the individual, the concept of enumeration of individuals, and the issue of person versus individual.

The Person as a Complex of Qualities Possessed by the Individual

Zizioulas claims that a person cannot be described as a complex of qualities possessed by the individual, because a person is something unique, but no biological, moral or social quality can be said to be unique. Nevertheless, the understanding of a person as a collection, congress or complex of properties is found in the Cappadocian texts when the Fathers try to explain what a person is. The notion of an individual human being as a collection of properties can be traced back quite clearly to Porphyry, although there are earlier hints of it in Plato and Plotinus as well.[16] Porphyry deals with this issue in the *Isagoge*, an introductory handbook of logic he wrote at the request of Chrysaorius, a Roman senator, who had studied Aristotle's *Categories* with little success and was asking for help. In this work Porphyry describes an individual human being, Socrates, as a unique collection of properties which in themselves are not unique. He writes:

> Socrates, this white, and this approaching son of Sophroniscus, if Socrates be his only son, are called individual (ἄτομον). Such things are called individuals because each thing is composed of a collection of properties which can never be the same for another; for the properties of Socrates could not be the same for any other particular man. The properties of man, however, I mean the man in common, will be the same for a great many, more strongly, for all particular men as men.[17]

In describing Socrates as a collection of properties, Porphyry uses individual qualities ("this white"), individual relations ("this approaching son of Sophroniscus") and individual substances ("Socrates") to describe an individual. If one were to use Aristotelian language, one should say that Porphyry uses individual categories, both substances and accidents, to describe an individual.

It is quite likely that the Cappadocians were familiar with the definition of an individual as a collection of properties, since in Basil of Caesarea's *Adversus Eunomium* 2,4 and Gregory of Nyssa's *Diff. ous. hyp.* 3 we see the example of Socrates being replaced with that of the Apostle Peter and Job, respectively, who are both described as unique collections of properties. In both passages, the authors try to distinguish substance from individuals. Thus, Basil describes Peter as the son of Jonah, born in Bethsaida, the brother of Andrew, and the first one called to the apostolic ministry; he adds that none of these properties is his substance. If the latter statement is put in a positive fashion and the Aristotelian terminology is preserved, these properties are said to be accidents.

Gregory explains that the Bible describes Job as "this man" (that is, a particular human) and then adds his peculiar notes, designating the place where he lives (the land of Uz), the marks which reveal his character (truthful, blameless, righteous, fearing God, and avoiding evil), and all such external adjuncts that differentiate him and set him apart from the common notion of human (having ten children, seven thousand sheep, etc.). The description of the person named Job suggests that this person is individualized by putting together some of his characteristic marks, a conclusion confirmed by Gregory himself when he writes: "a person (ὑπόστασις) is also the concourse of the peculiar characteristics."[18]

Even if, as John Rist has convincingly shown,[19] Basil knew very little Plotinus, we have to accept that he perhaps read Porphyry's *Isagoge* or a handbook that reproduced Porphyry's arguments. And so quite likely did Gregory of Nyssa, since he perhaps used his brother's library.[20] The *Isagoge* can be used as a beginner's guide to Aristotle's *Categories* and, given its introductory purpose, the *Isagoge*'s arguments are less sophisticated than the arguments Porphyry provides in his other Aristotelian commentaries. What is perhaps most important is that the particular doctrine of an individual as a collection of properties does not occur in such a clear formulation in any extant pagan writing (still less in Christian writings!) prior to the *Isagoge*. Therefore, the Cappadocians and later Neoplatonists might have been fascinated by it and adopted it in their writings.

It thus becomes clear that a Neoplatonic influence on two Cappadocian Fathers makes them understand a person as a collection of properties, a possibility which Zizioulas does not seem to be aware of, let alone considers with care.

The Concept of Enumeration of Individuals

Another issue Zizioulas disavows is that of the individual being partial, because it is subject to addition and combination, whereas a person is free from such boundaries of the "self" as individualization, comprehension, combination, definition, description and use. Here I deal with the issue of individual being subject to addition and combination in Gregory of Nyssa. For the Cappadocian Fathers, the concept of enumeration of individuals (that is, individuals being subject to addition and combination) was an important feature of the concept of person. They were concerned with how to distinguish between the three divine persons and the divine substance. To do so, Gregory of Nyssa, for example, argues that unlike substance which cannot be enumerated, individuals sharing the same substance (or nature) can be counted. *Ad Ablabium* is one of the works where Gregory uses this argument. In this short treatise (already treated in detail in this volume by Lewis Ayres), Ablabius, a friend who does not know how to understand the formula "one substance, three hypostases", confronts Gregory with two equally extreme alternatives: either say "three gods" or speak of one God, excluding the Son and the Spirit from the divinity. The former alternative is Tritheism, whereas the latter is extreme Arianism and Macedonianism. Ablabius asks: If we can speak of Peter, James, and John as *three humans* although they are one in nature, why not speak of three gods also? In other words, if it is logical to refer to humans, who are more than one, by the plural number of the name derived from their nature, why then is this absurd in the divine case? Gregory launches himself in an argument about the meaning of the words "human" and "God", explaining that those words do in fact refer to the human and divine nature respectively, which in themselves are one. Therefore, it is incorrect, or an abuse of language, to speak of many humans or many gods. Nevertheless, Gregory has to recognize that common language employs the phrase "many humans", as does the Scripture. Hence he is constrained to say that we can actually tolerate this bad habit in the case of the lower nature, "since no harm results from the mistaken use of the name".[21] Yet, the same variation in the use of the term is not acceptable in the case of the divine nature.[22] First of all, the habit of calling "many" that which is one is dangerous in referring to the divine, because it contravenes the Scripture: "Hear, O Israel, the Lord your God is one Lord" (Deut. 6:4).

Moreover, he takes this opportunity to make even clearer the distinction between substance and persons. For that purpose, he uses the notion of the enumeration of individuals. In *Ad Ablabium* 40, 24ff. Gregory writes: "the notion of persons admits of that separation which is made by the peculiar attributes observed in each severally, and when they are combined is presented to us by means of number." To make this theoretical explanation more accessible to Ablabius, Gregory puts forward several concrete examples. He says that we do not speak of "many golds" but of "much gold". Yet, we do speak of "many gold pieces" or "gold coins", or "staters", without finding any multiplication of the nature of gold by the number of staters;[23] but after making this statement, he emends it by saying that "properly, we should not call them 'gold [coins]' but 'golden [coins]'".[24] Similarly, continues Gregory, one can think of Peter and James, and John as many, "yet the human [nature] in them is one".[25] Elsewhere, Gregory writes that "Numerical order does not bring about diversity of the natures, but the numbered items, whatever their nature is, remain what they are, whether they are numbered or not. The number is a sign to make it known how many things are."[26] Basil of Caesarea also uses the concept of enumeration of hypostases (by hypostasis he means person here),[27] but he insists that the divine hypostases have to be "enumerated piously" (εὐσεβῶς ἀριθμεῖν) not materially and adds that divinity is above number.[28] The concept of enumeration of individuals is another feature of the Cappadocian concept of person of which Zizioulas is unaware.

Person vs. Individual
As presented above, Zizioulas is very bothered by the understanding of a person as an individual. He attributes this development to Augustine and Boethius. I do not intend to analyze whether Boethius's and Augustine's views are portrayed accurately in this account as being at the root of the problem; Orthodox theologians generally do not study the Latin Fathers, and Zizioulas is a specialist in neither of the above.[29] The distinction between individual and person is certainly necessary in our time, because of the negative connotations individualism has acquired. When criticizing individualism, Zizioulas most likely had in mind the political and social philosophy of individualism "that places high value on the freedom of the individual and generally stresses the self-directed, self-contained, and comparatively unrestrained individual or ego".[30] Yet, that philosophy was not present at the time of the Cappadocians. They were using person interchangeably with individual and did not have any problem with that. Theirs was a time when the notion of individual/person was only emerging. They were faced with other problems, trying to distinguish between substance (or nature) and person. As one can see from studying the trinitarian controversies of the fourth century CE, many theologians had trouble understanding that distinction, especially since ὑπόστασις, one of the Greek words used for person, also meant substance.

Let me exemplify with Gregory of Nyssa's *Ad Graecos*. The complete title of this work is the following: "By stating 'three persons' in the Godhead, we do not say 'three gods'. To the Greeks, based on common notions."[31] In *Ad Graecos*, Gregory wants to prove that, even if one bases one's understanding of God on the "common notions" and not on revelation, one cannot infer that there are three gods from the fact that Christians speak of three persons in the Godhead. By "common notions" (κοιναὶ ἐννοίαι) Gregory means "general principles" or "universally accepted opinions". Basil of Caesarea, too, in a polemical context against Eunomius says that the κοιναὶ ἐννοίαι tell us that God exists, not *what* he is.[32] The Stoic doctrine of the "common notions" was widespread in ancient philosophy and was used to establish a ground of common agreement as a support for a given theory.[33] "The Greeks" referred to in the title were perhaps contemporaries who were trained in Greek philosophy and could not accept that God is triune.

In his *Ad Graecos*, most of the time Gregory uses πρόσωπον and ὑπόστασις synonymously when referring to divine and human persons; but whereas the former term occurs sixty times, the later only occurs thirty-six times. He also uses ὑπόστασις to refer to a horse (!). To express the notion of the person, however, he also uses other terms, such as "individual or indivisible" (ἄτομον), "partial substance" (μερικὴ οὐσία), and "particular substance" (ἰδικὴ οὐσία).

Here is one of the passages where he makes it clear that a person is an individual: "If somebody says that we call Peter and Paul and Barnabas three partial substances (οὐσίας μερικάς) (it is clear that this means particular (ἰδικάς) [substances])—for this is more accurate to say—he should recognize that [by that] we do not mean anything else but the individual, which is the person (ἄτομον, ὅπερ ἐστὶ πρόσωπον)."[34]

Elsewhere in the same treatise Gregory states that another word used for person, namely "hypostasis", can be understood as "individual". He writes "it is clear that species (εἶδος) and individual (ἄτομον) are not the same thing, that is, substance [is not the same] as hypostasis".[35] "Individual", continues Gregory, that is hypostasis, makes one think of someone with curly hair, gray eyes, a father, a son and the like, whereas the term "species", that is substance, makes one think of "a rational animal, mortal, capable of understanding and knowledge" or of "an irrational animal, mortal, capable of neighing and the like".[36] He then applies the same reasoning by analogy to God. The reader of Gregory's explanations is supposed to have understood by now that the three divine persons have the same common substance and that the relation between the substance and the persons is the same as that between a species and its individuals.[37] The above two texts clearly show, in my view, that Gregory was not reluctant to use "individual" (in the sense of something "indivisible") and "person" interchangeably, against Zizioulas's contention.

Possible Modern Influences on Zizioulas

Having attempted to demonstrate that Zizioulas does not know his Cappadocian theology well, I think it is perhaps in order to investigate briefly which modern thinkers possibly influenced him. It is probably a good idea to start by considering what a Catholic admirer of Zizioulas, Catherine Mowry LaCugna, had to say about his views of person. One of her books helps to map out our route through Zizioulas's sources. Although an admirer of Zizioulas and clearly influenced by his views of person—especially his fascination with person as a relational entity and the alleged primacy of the person over substance in Cappadocian theology[38]—in her highly controversial book *God for Us*, LaCugna was able to see some of Zizioulas's weak points and to propose a more comprehensive concept of person. She contends that a person cannot be defined *only* in relation with others (heteronomy),[39] but that a person has her or his intrinsic value (autonomy) apart from the relations with others. She uses the example of an unborn child, who is not an "agent" in Macmurray's sense—that is, one who is capable of acting intentionally—nor is it baptized in Zizioulas's sense—according to the latter, a baptized person is capable of reaching the fullness of personhood. According to LaCugna, "The unborn may 'exist' before anyone (mother; physician) is even aware of it and consciously in relation to it. If persons are constituted entirely by their relations, or entirely by their ecclesial incorporation, this would theoretically at least make it possible to justify the position that a woman who refuses to be in relation to an unborn is refusing to endow it with personhood." Therefore, LaCugna concludes that heteronomy needs to be balanced with autonomy when defining a person.[40]

LaCugna was aware that the contemporary understanding of person as a relational entity has been a more recent discovery. [41] In the eighteenth and nineteenth centuries "in reaction to the atomism and solipsism of critical philosophy, new currents of thought had arisen in science, philosophy, and psychology that emphasized the social and relational character of person-hood and indeed of all reality". In the twentieth century process philosophy, Sartrean existentialism, French phenomenology, Wittgensteinian language analysis, and personalist philosophies, all sought to "go beyond the dual-ism and individualism of the Cartesian tradition by giving priority to inter-action and participation as modes of being and knowing". The personalist philosophies of Jewish thinkers such as Martin Buber, Franz Rosenzweig, and Felix Ebner all presented themselves as an alternative to the Cartesian and Lockean understanding of person as an individual center of conscious-ness. LaCugna bases some of the above observations on a very informative article on "Person" written by Pannenberg,[42] the same article Zizioulas him-self quoted as early as 1976.[43]

While it is difficult to pinpoint which modern author may have influenced Zizioulas's view of person, it is plausible to conjecture that some of those he mentions approvingly did perhaps influence him. In his 1976 article, "Human Capacity and Human Incapacity: A Theological Exploration of Personhood", Zizioulas mentions approvingly several western thinkers, such as Martin Buber, John Macmurray, Wolfhart Pannenberg, and David Jenkins, all of whom have understood a person as a relational category. The latter group of westerners' concept of person appears to be in sharp contrast with the Boethian-Augustinian individualistic tradition referred to initially by Zizioulas as being characteristic of the western mindset. I shall therefore suggest that Buber and Macmurray are the most likely to have influenced Zizioulas's concept of person.

Buber taught, following, as he claimed, a suggestion of the nineteenth-century German philosopher Ludwig Feuerbach,[44] that a human can only realize himself or herself as a human being in a relation with another, who may be another human or God. In his celebrated *I and Thou* (first published in German in 1923), Buber introduces the notion of relation which helps to distinguish between individual and person in terms highly reminiscent of Zizioulas, as already quoted earlier. "Individuality", writes Buber, "makes its appearance by being different from other individualities. A person makes his appearance by entering into relation with other persons".[45] It is known that Buber's thinking moved from mysticism to dialogue. While in earlier writings (e.g., *Daniel*, 1913) he advocated the notion of a mystical union between humans and God, in *I and Thou* he embraced the notion of their encounter, which presupposes and preserves their separate existence. According to this view, God is the absolute Person, the great Thou. God is "him who—whatever else he may be—enters into a direct relation with us men in creative, revealing and redeeming acts, and thus makes it possible for us to enter into a direct relation with him".[46] A true relationship with God, as experienced from the human side, must be an I-Thou relationship, in which God is truly met and addressed, not merely thought of and expressed.[47] This great Thou is also the one who enables relations between humans and other beings.

In moving from Buber to Macmurray, I agree with LaCugna's observation about the two thinkers: "Buber suggests something quite close to Macmurray's idea that the self-as-subject is a nonexistent, or at least the negative of true selfhood, when Buber notes that the I must become actual through its participation in the other."[48] For Macmurray the personal is constituted by the relation of persons;[49] the self is fundamentally relational, the outcome of a person's ongoing relational history. The example LaCugna used about the mother and the child (to point to the fact that a child is not only a relational person), was actually first offered by Macmurray. Yet, unlike LaCugna, Macmurray offers this example to illustrate how the child is a relational person who will not survive without personal relationships.[50] The texts and ideas I chose from Buber and Macmurray are clearly reminiscent of some of Zizioulas's ideas. Therefore, it is likely that Zizioulas has borrowed some elements from Buber's and Macmurray's concept of person,[51] attempting to shape his own concept of person. But the main difference between Zizioulas, on the one hand, and Buber and Macmurray on the other hand, is that Zizioulas has tried to give his concept of relational person a normative Greek patristic content.

Conclusion

To sum up, I hope this article has proven that, despite claiming that his own ontology of personhood is patristic-based, Zizioulas has not convincingly exegeted the Cappadocian theology of person, especially that of Gregory of Nyssa and Basil of Caesarea. This is unfortunate, given the fact that there are dozens of patristic quotations from, or references to, various Greek Fathers (especially the Cappadocians) throughout Zizioulas's works. Instead, he uses nineteenth- and twentieth-century insights which he then foists on the Cappadocians. This methodology leads him to misleading conclusions. Unlike contemporary thinkers, the Cappadocian Fathers were not aware of the dangers of individualism and perhaps that is why they did not make many efforts to distinguish between person and individual. They were more concerned with distinguishing between person or individual, on the one hand, and nature or substance, on the other hand, in connection with the Christian

God. At that time, the three divine persons were not properly understood as three different entities while each was one and the same God. Some also believed that there was only one divine person, the person of the Father— the Son and the Holy Spirit were created—while others posited three gods. Moreover, the Cappadocians were not interested in personalism per se, but in defending the Holy Trinity. Zizioulas is therefore in error when he contends that the Cappadocians did not understand a person as an individual or when he credits them with having had the same concerns we moderns have when combating individualism today.

NOTES

1   C. C. J. Webb, *God and Personality* (New York, NY: Macmillan, 1918); J. E. Walgrave, *Person and Society: A Christian View* (Pittsburgh, PA: Duquesne University Press, 1965); P. F. Strawson, *Individuals: An Essay in Descriptive Metaphysics* (London: Routledge, 1964).
2   Other theologians have also written on the topic: Leonardo Boff, *Trinity and Society* (Maryknoll, NY: Orbis Books, 1988); Patricia Wilson-Kastner, *Faith, Feminism and the Christ* (Philadelphia, PA: Fortress Press, 1983); Colin E. Gunton, *The Promise of Trinitarian Theology*, 2d ed. (Edinburgh: T. & T. Clark, 1997); Christos Yannaras, *The Freedom of Morality* (Crestwood, NY: St. Vladimir's Seminary Press, 1984); Catherine Mowry LaCugna, *God for Us: The Trinity and Christian Life* (San Francisco, CA: Harper, 1991).
3   This insight was cogently summarized by Sarah Coakley, "Why Three? Some Further Reflections on the Origins of the Doctrine of the Trinity", in *The Making and Remaking of Christian Doctrine*, (eds) S. Coakley and D. A. Pailin (Oxford: Oxford University Press, 1993), pp. 35–36. Cf. also Stanley Rudman, *Concepts of Person and Christian Ethics* (Cambridge: Cambridge University Press, 1997), pp. 171–189.
4   John Zizioulas, "The Teaching of the 2nd Ecumenical Council on the Holy Spirit in Historical and Ecumenical Perspective", in *Credo in Spiritum Sanctum: atti del Congresso teologico internazionale di pneumatologia in occasione del 1600 anniversario del I Concilio di Costantinopoli e del 1550o anniversario de Concilio di Efeso, Roma, 22–26 marzo 1982* , (ed) Jose Saraiva Martins (Vatican City: Libreria Editrice Vaticana, 1983), p. 36
5   John Zizioulas, *Being as Communion: Studies in Personhood and the Church* (Crestwood, NY: St. Vladimir's Seminary Press, 1985).
6   For a similar view, see Rudman, *Concepts of Person*, p. 129.
7   John Zizioulas, "Human Capacity and Human Incapacity: A Theological Exploration of Personhood", *Scottish Journal of Theology* 28, no. 5 (1975), p. 407.
8   John Zizioulas, *Being as Communion*, p. 47.
9   John Zizioulas, "On Being a Person. Towards an Ontology of Personhood", in *Persons, Divine and Human. King's College Essays in Theological Anthropology*, (eds) Christoph Schwöbel and Colin E. Gunton (Edinburgh: T. & T. Clark, 1991), p. 45. Cf. also *Being as Communion*, p. 47.
10 Zizioulas, "Human Capacity", pp. 408, 410–411.
11 Zizioulas, *Being as Communion*, p. 47.
12 Zizioulas, "Human Capacity", pp. 405f.
13 Zizioulas, "Human Capacity", p. 442. Cf. also Zizioulas, "On Being a Person", p. 41.
14 Zizioulas, *Being as Communion*, p. 46.
15 Zizioulas, *Being as Communion*, p. 46.
16 Plato, *Theaetetus* 157b–c; Plotinus, *Enneads* VI.3.8.20, VI.3.10.16, VI.3.15.27.
17 Porphyry the Phoenician, *Isagoge*, 7, 20–26, trans. Edward W. Warren (Toronto: Pontifical Institute of Mediaeval Studies, 1975), p. 41. Greek text in Porphyry, *Isagoge et In Aristotelis Categorias Comentarium* 7, 20–26, (ed) Adolf Busse, Commentaria in Aristotelem Graeca 4.1 (Berlin: Reimer, 1887).
18 Gregory of Nyssa, *diff. ous. hyp.* 6. 4–6: τὴν συνδρομὴν τῶν ἰδιωμάτων. Cf. Volker H. Drecoll, *Die Entwicklung der Trinitätslehre des Basilius von Cäsarea: Sein Weg vom Homöusianer zum Neonizäner* (Göttingen: Vandenhoeck & Ruprecht, 1996), p. 317. Greek text of this letter in

Saint Basil, *Lettres*, text established and translated by Yves Courtonne, vol. 1 (Paris: Les Belles Lettres, 1957), pp. 81–92. I also consulted an English translation of this letter, St. Basil, *The Letters*, trans. Roy J. Deferrari, vol. 1 (London: W. Heinemann, 1926); however, since Deferrari's translation is not too reliable, I had to alter it.

19   John M. Rist, "Basil's 'Neoplatonism': Its Background and Nature" in *Basil of Caesarea: Christian, Humanist, Ascetic. A Sixteenth-Hundredth Anniversary Symposium*, (ed) Paul J. Fedwick, vol. 1 (Toronto: Pontifical Institute of Medieval Studies, 1981), pp. 137–220.

20   Speaking of Gregory of Nyssa's Platonism in a recent article, Rist allows that "further investigation of the indirect effects of Porphyry might alter this picture in some details" (John M. Rist, "Plotinus and Christian Philosophy" in *The Cambridge Companion to Plotinus*, (ed) Lloyd P. Gerson [Cambridge: Cambridge University Press, 1996], p. 401).

21   Gregory of Nyssa, *Ad Ablabium* 41, 18ff. Greek text in *Ad Ablabium Quod non sint tres dei* in *Gregorii Nysseni Opera*, vol. 3, part 1, (ed) Friedrich Müller (Leiden: E. J. Brill, 1958), pp. 35–58. For an English translation I consulted the Gregory of Nyssa, *On "Not Three Gods". To Ablabius*, in *Select Writings and Letters of Gregory, Bishop of Nyssa*, trans. H. A. Wilson in NPNF, 2d series, vol. 5 (New York, NY: The Christian Literature Company, 1893), pp. 331–336; yet, since the latter predates the critical edition prepared by Müller, I did not rely entirely on it.

22   *Ad Ablabium* 42, 1–3.

23   *Ad Ablabium* 53, 16ff.

24   *Ad Ablabium* 53, 25–54, 1.

25   *Ad Ablabium* 54, 2f.

26   Gregory of Nyssa, *Contra Eunomium* I, 201–201. Greek text in *Contra Eunomium Libri* in *Gregorii Nysseni Opera*, vols. 1–2, (ed) Werner Jaeger (Leiden: E. J. Brill, 1960). An English translation of the whole work predating Jaeger's critical edition can be found in *Select Writings and Letters of Gregory, Bishop of Nyssa*, NPNF, 2d series, vol. 5 (New York, NY: The Christian Literature Company, 1893), pp. 33–315. A more recent English translation in *Contra Eunomium* I by Stuart George Hall is found in *El "Contra Eunomium I" en la produccion literaria de Gregorio de Nisa. Sixth International Colloquium on Gregory of Nyssa*, (eds) Lucas F. Mateo-Seco and Juan L. Bastero (Pamplona: Universidad de Navarra, 1988), pp. 21–135.

27   Basil of Caesarea, *Ep.* 210, 5. 31–36 (Courtonne 2:195–6), *Ep.* 214, 4. 16–22 (Courtonne 2:205–206). For the meaning of ὑπόστασις in these letters, see Lucian Turcescu, "Prosopon and Hypostasis in Basil of Caesarea's *Against Eunomius* and the Epistles", *Vigiliae Christianae* 51, no. 4 (1997), pp. 389–394.

28   *De Spiritu Sancto* 18, 44. 1–23 ((ed) Pruche, 402–404, Sources chretiennes 17 bis). Cf. Andrea Milano, *Persona in teologia. Alle origini del significato di persona nel cristianesimo antico* (Naples: Dehoniane, 1984), pp. 149–151. Troiano traces the concept of enumeration of hypostases back to Aristotle's *Met.* 1074a31–38 (Marina Silvia Troiano, "Il concetto di numerazione delle ipostasi in Basilio di Cesarea", *Vetera Christianorum* 24 (1987), pp. 350f.).

29   For person in Boethius, see the excellent treatment by Sean Mulrooney, "Boethius on 'Person'", (Ph.D dissertation, University of Toronto, 1994). For person in Augustine, see A. C. Lloyd, "On Augustine's Concept of a Person", in *Augustine: A Collection of Critical Essays*, (ed) Robert A Markus (New York, NY: Anchor Books, 1972), pp. 191–205; William R. O'Connor, "The Concept of the Person in St. Augustine's *De Trinitate*", *Augustinian Studies* 13 (1982), pp. 133–144; Hubertus R. Drobner, *Person-Exegese und Christologie bei Augustinus: Zur Herkunft der Formel Una persona* (Leiden: E. J. Brill, 1986); John M. Rist, "What Will I Be Like Tomorrow? Augustine versus Hume", *American Catholic Philosophical Quarterly* 74 no. 1 (2000), pp. 95–114.

30   "Individualism", in *Encyclopedia Britannica* online at http://www.britannica.com/bcom/ eb/article/printable/0/0,5722,43280,00.html/.

31   References to the Greek text will be to *Ad Graecos (ex communibus notionibus)* in *Gregorii Nysseni Opera*, vol. 3, part 1, (ed) Friedrich Müller (Leiden: E. J. Brill, 1958), pp. 17–34. The English translation of the passages quoted is mine. Cf. also Gregory of Nyssa, "*Ad Graecos*: How It Is that We Say There Are Three Persons in the Divinity but Do Not Say that There Are Three Gods" (To the Greeks: Concerning the Commonality of Concepts), trans. Daniel F. Stramara, Jr, *The Greek Orthodox Theological Review* 41, no. 4 (1996), pp. 381–391.

32   Basil of Caesarea, *Adversus Eunomium* 1, 12.8 (Sources chrétiennes 299:212). Cf. R. P. C. Hanson, *The Search for the Christian Doctrine of God: The Arian Controversy 318–381* (Edinburgh: T. & T. Clark, 1988), pp. 689f.

33 See Robert B. Todd, "The Stoic Common Notions: A Re-Examination and Reinterpretation", *Symbolae Osloenses* 48 (1973), pp. 47–75.
34 *Ad Graecos* 23, 4–8. Cf. Johannes Zachhuber, *Human Nature in Gregory of Nyssa: Philosophical Background and Theological Significance* (Leiden: E. J. Brill, 2000), p. 111.
35 *Ad Graecos* 31, 1–2.
36 *Ad Graecos* 31, 2–7.
37 *Ad Graecos* 32, 21–26.
38 For an excellent dismantling of the latter paradigm introduced by the nineteenth-century Jesuit theologian Théodore de Régnon, see André de Halleux, "Personnalisme ou essentialisme trinitaire chez les Pères cappadociens? Une mauvaise controverse", *Revue théologique de Louvain* 17 (1986), pp. 129–155 and 265–292; idem, "'Hypostase' et 'personne' dans la formation du dogme trinitaire (ca. 375–381)", *Revue d'histoire ecclésiastique* 79 (1984), pp. 313–369, 625–670. Another critic of the paradigm, Michel Barnes, is concerned to show that most twentieth-century English language scholarship dealing with the Trinity takes de Régnon's paradigm as an axiom, without being aware of its nineteenth-century scholastic origin; see Michel René Barnes, "De Régnon Reconsidered", *Augustinian Studies* 26 (1995), pp. 51–79; idem, "Augustine in Contemporary Trinitarian Theology", *Theological Studies* 56 (1995), pp. 237–250; cf. also John G. F. Wilks, "The Trinitarian Ontology of John Zizioulas", *Vox Evangelica* 25 (1995), pp. 63–88.
39 Zizioulas wrote "We can understand [the person] only as *schesis*" [that is, relation] ("Human Capacity", p. 436).
40 LaCugna, *God for Us*, p. 310.
41 LaCugna, *God for Us*, p. 255.
42 W. Pannenberg, "Person", *Die Religion in Geschichte und Gegenwart: Handwörterbuch für Theologie und Religionswissenschaft*, third edition vol. 5 (Tübingen: J. C. B. Mohr, 1957–1965), pp. 230–234.
43 Zizioulas, "Human Capacity", p. 408, n. 1.
44 "Jewish Philosophy", in *Encyclopedia Britannica* online at http://www.britannica.com/bcom/eb/article/6/0,5716,108156+27+105859,00.html/.
45 Martin Buber, *I and Thou*, second ed., trans. Ronald G. Smith (New York, NY: Charles Scribner's Sons, 1958), p. 62. Cf. Zizioulas, "Human Capacity", p. 442 and Zizioulas, "On Being a Person", p. 41.
46 Buber, *I and Thou*, p. 135.
47 "Buber, Martin", in *The New Encyclopedia Britannica*, vol. 2, fifteenth edition (Chicago, IL: Encyclopedia Britannica, 1998).
48 LaCugna, *God for Us*, pp. 307f. Martin Buber, *I and Thou* and John Macmurray, *Persons in Relation* (New York, NY: Harper, 1961), p. 24.
49 Macmurray, *Persons in Relation*, p. 51.
50 Ibid.
51 In his "Human Capacity" (p. 408), Zizioulas mentions Buber's *I and Thou* and John Macmurray's *Persons in Relations* and *The Self as Agent*. Zizioulas mentions Buber again in *Being as Communion*, p. 17.

The research and writing of this article was supported by a St. Francis Xavier University Research grant. I would like to thank my university for its support.

7

THE MIRROR OF THE INFINITE: GREGORY OF NYSSA ON THE *VESTIGIA TRINITATIS*

DAVID BENTLEY HART

I

The notion that, from the patristic period to the present, the Trinitarian theologies of the Eastern and Western catholic traditions have obeyed contrary logics and have in consequence arrived at conclusions inimical each to the other—a particularly tedious, persistent, and pernicious falsehood—will no doubt one day fade away from want of documentary evidence. At present, however, it serves too many interests for theological scholarship to dispense with it too casually: Eastern theologians find in it a weapon to wield against the West, which they believe has traditionally—so alleges, for instance, John Zizioulas—forgotten the biblical truth that the unity of the Trinity flows from the paternal *arche*, which is entirely "personal", and come to believe instead "that that which constitutes the unity of God is the one divine substance, the one divinity";[1] Western theologians of varying hues—quasi-Hegelian dialectical Trinitarians, social Trinitarians, "personalist" theologians—take it as a license for their differing critiques of the "Platonism" or "Hellenism" of classical Trinitarian metaphysics; and all of us who, in our weaker moments, prefer synopsis to precision find in it a convenient implement for arranging our accounts of doctrinal history into simple taxonomies, under tidily discrete divisions. It was, learned opinion generally concurs, Théodore de Régnon who probably first "discovered" the distinction between Western and Eastern styles of Trinitarian theology: the tendency, that is, of Latin thought to proceed from general nature to concrete Person (the latter as a mode of the former), so according priority to divine unity, and of Greek thought to proceed from Person to nature (the latter as the content

David Bentley Hart
Department of Theology, Loyola College, 4501 N. Charles Street, Baltimore, MD 21210, USA

of the former), so placing the emphasis first on the plurality of divine Persons.[2] Régnon's own aims, as it happens, were quite modest and eirenic, and he certainly understood that, in whatever degree his analysis was correct, neither East nor West enjoyed a manifestly better claim to dogmatic purity; but his distinction has served little purpose in recent years but to feed Eastern polemic and Western insecurity, and to distort the tradition that both share. Now we find ourselves in an age in which many of us have come to believe that we must choose between "Greek" personalism and "Latin" essentialism, or at least remain poised between them; and as a result we have become insensible to the subtlety and richness of the sources that have thus been subjected to these fairly arid categories.

The moment in ecclesial history at which the divergence between East and West on these matters supposedly became acute, at least according to the prevailing prejudices, was some time in the late fourth century and early fifth. This is supposedly especially obvious when one compares the Trinitarian theology of the Cappadocian fathers (particularly Gregory of Nyssa) to that of Augustine. Indeed, if one confines one's investigations to a few select texts, one can make something of a case here: did not Augustine, after all, refuse to draw an analogy of the Trinity from the relationship of husband, wife, and child,[3] favouring instead more elliptical analogies drawn from the mind's inner complexity; and did not Gregory, by contrast, go so far at one point as to defend Trinitarianism against the accusation of tritheism by arguing not only that it is incorrect to speak of three gods, but that it is only catachrestically that we speak even of three men, insofar as human nature is one?[4] But the contrast is no sooner drawn than it begins to melt away: Augustine, certainly, evinces no less keen a sense of the distinct integrity of the divine Persons as Persons than does Gregory,[5] nor does Gregory actually argue that the unity of the Trinity is reducible to a common nature wherein the divine Persons severally subsist (anyway—*vide infra*—Gregory's understanding of human "nature" is so splendidly peculiar as to make it impossible to draw any facile "social" conclusions from his argument); more to the point, in neither instance is either theologian actually attempting to provide a conceptual definition of the Trinity. We should perhaps do well to remember that it is one thing to move about in the realm of analogy, within which one merely seeks out locutions and similitudes by which creaturely language and thought can pass, however imperfectly, from created towards divine being; but it is another thing altogether to move in the far more mysterious realm of the *imago Dei*, where one must seek first not what we may say of God, but what God says of himself in fashioning us as the creatures we are, called from nothingness to participate in the being that flows from him, and to manifest his beauty in the depths of our nature. It is wise to keep this distinction constantly in view: for while Augustine and Gregory alike are quite willing to consider the many ways in which we may shape models of the Trinitarian relations in our words and reflections, both become rather more circumspect when attempting to identify precisely how the image of the triune God resides in us. It is precisely here, though—in contemplating where the image of God is impressed upon his creatures, and how—that Trinitarian reflection can achieve its fullest and supplest expression.

One should also note, at the outset, that for Gregory, no less than for Augustine, the divine image is first and foremost the possession of each individual soul, in the mystery of her simultaneous unity of essence and diversity of acts. For instance, Gregory, in *On the Making of Humanity*, explicitly rejects the suggestion that that most basic "form" of human sociality —the distinction between the sexes—is in any sense a feature of God's image in us: "for in Jesus Christ, according to the apostle, there is neither male nor female".[6] Rather, the image is more properly to be sought on the one hand in a variety of spiritual attributes inhering in the soul—reason, love, freedom— and on the other in the soul's simultaneous complexity and simplicity. Gregory is even willing to argue to the indivisibility of the Trinity from the indivisibility of the soul that is created in its image,[7] and then to argue back again, in the opposite direction, from the revealed nature of the Trinity to what constitutes God's image in us: God, scripture tells us, is Mind and Word, and so we possess word and understanding in imitation of the true Word and Mind; God is love, God beholds and hearkens to and searches out all things, and hence we love, and hence we see and hear and seek understanding.[8] Even the mind's transcendence of itself—our inability to grasp how, again, an intelligible and simple unity can subsist in a dynamic and versatile plurality of movements and capacities—is an aspect of the divine image in us, reflecting God's own incomprehensibility and hiddenness.[9] Nor should one assume that the soul's singularity of personal identity is, for Gregory, simply and solely a defect in its likeness to the triune God, or any more of a limitation upon that likeness than is the social constitution of creaturely personality; certainly Gregory, insofar as he ventures any portrayal of the interior life of God, does not elevate divine triplicity over divine unity, any more than the reverse:

> … the divine nature exceeds each [finite] good, and the good is wholly beloved by the good, and thus it follows that when it looks upon itself it desires what it possesses and possesses what it desires (ὃ ἔχει, θέλει, καὶ ὃ θέλει, ἔχει), and receives nothing from outside itself. … the life of that transcendent nature is love, in that the beautiful is entirely lovable to those who know it (and God does know it), and so this knowledge becomes love (ἡ δὲ γνῶσις ἀγάπη γίνεται), because the object of his recognition is in its nature beautiful.[10]

It is all but impossible to read such a passage without discerning in it an essentially Trinitarian grammar. Surely this progression—from the divine nature's infinite source, through God's *gnosis* of himself, to the "conversion" of that recognition into delighted love, into *agape*—is a description of how the one God, even in his infinite simplicity, eternally conceives his equally infinite image, knowing himself perfectly in his Logos, and so eternally "wills" himself with an equally infinite love, so completing his Trinitarian life in the movement of the Spirit. This is, after all, entirely in keeping with the venerable Cappadocian insight that in God—*ad extra* and so, necessarily, *ad intra*[11]—all is inaugurated in the Father, effected in the Son, and perfected in the Spirit.

Morphologically, at least, this account of the simplicity of God's nature as also an infinitely accomplished act of knowledge and love—or as the perfect coincidence of desire and possession—entirely follows the logic of Gregory's (and Basil's)[12] belief that the generation of the Son is directly from the Father, while the procession of the Spirit is from the Father only *per Filium* (*sed*, to borrow a phrase, *de Patre principaliter*). Admittedly, Gregory does not, in the passage just quoted, make an explicit connection between God's infinite immanent act of knowing and loving his own essence and the *taxis* of the Trinity; but Augustine does:

> ... the Son is from the Father, so as both to be and to be coeternal with the Father. For if the image perfectly fills the measure of him whose image it is, then it is coequal to its source ... He has, in regard to this image, employed the name "form" on account, I believe, of its beauty, wherein there is at once such harmony, and prime equality, and prime similitude, in no way discordant, in no measure unequal, and in no part dissimilar, but wholly answering to the identity of the one whose image it is ... Wherefore that ineffable conjunction of the Father and his image is never without fruition, without love, without rejoicing. Hence that love, delight, felicity, or beatitude, if any human voice can worthily say it, is called by him, in brief, use, and is in the Trinity the Holy Spirit, not begotten, but of the begetter and begotten alike the very sweetness, filling all creatures, according to their capacities, with his bountiful super-abundance and excessiveness ... In that Trinity is the highest origin of all things, and the most perfect beauty, and the most blessed delight. Therefore those three are seen to be mutually determined, and are in themselves infinite.[13]

Clearly, at any rate, for both theologians the simplicity of God's essence and the distinctness of his internal relations are to be held together, however imponderable the ultimate convertibility of these things must remain for the finite mind. This oscillation between the poles of the one and the three is constantly present in the thought of both. One sees it, to take an example almost at random, in Gregory's remark that "if the Father wills something, the Son, being in the Father, knows the Father's will—or, rather, the Son himself is the Father's will";[14] or in his statement that "just as a man's spirit within him and the man himself are one man, even so God's Spirit within him and God himself should truly be called the one, first, and sole God".[15]

And both Gregory and Augustine resolve the aporia that theology must thus inevitably confront not by depicting the Trinity as a social "event" accomplished by three independent subjectivities, but in terms of the order of relations that distinguish the Persons from one another "causally" within the absolute simplicity of the divine nature. Both even distinguish generation and procession within the Trinity in terms primarily of the order of cause —as one perhaps must, unless one wishes to compromise the simplicity of the Father's essence by positing within God two acts that are separate and *essentially* different, rather than distinguished from one another relationally. As Gregory writes (in a passage that would fit very well in, say, Book V of Augustine's *De Trinitate*),

> ... while confessing the immutability of the [divine] nature, we do not deny difference in regard to cause and that which is caused, by which alone we discern the difference of each Person from the other, in that we believe one to be the cause and another to be from the cause; and again we conceive of another difference within that which is from the cause: between the one who, on the one hand, comes directly from the principle and the one who, on the other, comes from the principle through the one who arises directly; thus it unquestionably remains peculiar to the Son to be the Only Begotten, while at the same time it is not to be doubted that the Spirit is of the Father, by virtue of the mediation of the Son that safeguards the Son's character as Only Begotten, and thus the Spirit is not excluded from his natural relation to the Father.[16]

None of which is to say that for Gregory there is no relationship between the image of God in us and our nature as creatures necessarily in communion with one another (in a very striking way, as will be seen, some such relationship lies at the heart of his understanding of creation and redemption); nor is it to say, in the narrow terms to which modern theology occasionally succumbs, that Gregory's Trinitarian theology is "psychologistic" rather than "social", or that he accords the unity of the divine essence priority over the distinction of the divine Persons. Such oppositions are simply inapposite to classical Trinitarian theology, and are conceptually crude in any event. Surely, to indulge in something of an excursus, we must be acutely conscious of the analogical interval within those words—such as "person"—that we apply to both God and creatures, and always recall that the moral and ontological categories in which human personality are properly described are appropriate only to the finite and composite. The relationality of human persons, however essential it may be, remains a multiple reality, which must be described now in social terms, now in psychological, now in metaphysical; it is infinitely remote from that perfect indwelling, reciprocal "containment", transparency, recurrence, and absolute "giving way" that is the meaning of the word περιχώρησις or *circumincessio* (adopted by Trinitarian theology long after Gregory or Augustine, and yet so perfectly suited to the theology of both). For if we forget this interval, we not only risk lapsing into either a collectivistic or solipsistic reduction of human relationality—exclusively outward or inward—but we are likely to adopt either a tritheistic or a unitarian idiom when speaking of God. Our being is synthetic and bounded; just as (again to borrow a later theological vocabulary) the dynamic inseparability but incommensurability in us of essence and existence is an ineffably distant analogy of the dynamic identity of essence and existence in God, the constant pendulation between inner and outer that constitutes our identities is an ineffably distant analogy of that boundless bright diaphaneity of coinherence, in which the exteriority of relations and interiority of identity in God are one, each Person wholly reflecting and containing and indwelling each of the others. Because for us personality is synthetic, composite, successive, and finite, we are related always in some sense "over against", in a fragmentary way, and to be with others always involves for us a kind of death, the limit of our being. In God, though, given the simplicity of his essence, there is an absolute coincidence of relation and unity. For God, the "inwardness" of the other is each Person's own inwardness, the "outwardness" of the other is each Person's outwardness and manifestation.

It is precisely here that the artificial distinction between "Greek" and "Latin" theology has worked the most injurious mischief, by prompting many to rush to one end or the other of a scale that must be kept in balance. We must say, at once, that the divine simplicity is the "result" of the self-giving transparency and openness of infinite Persons, but also that the distinction of the Persons within the one God is the "result" of the infinite simplicity of the divine essence.[17] Otherwise, we will find ourselves trading in mythology: speaking of God as an infinite psychological subjectivity possessed of plural affects, or as a confederacy of three individual centres of consciousness; in either case reducing God, the transcendent source of all being, to a composite being, an ontic God, in whose "subjectivity" there would remain, even within the immanent divine life, some sort of unexpressed interiority (or interiorities), some surfeit of the indeterminate over the determinate, some reserve of self in which identity is constituted as the withheld. God is one because each divine Person, in the circle of God's knowledge and love of his own goodness (which is both wisdom and charity), is a "face", a "capture", of the divine essence that is—as must be, given the infinite simplicity of God—always wholly God, in the full depth of his "personality". For any "mode of subsistence" of the infinite being of God must be an infinite mode, a way whereby God is entirely, "personally" God. God is never less than wholly God. Just as the Father is the plenitude of divine goodness, in whom inhere both his Word (manifestation, form) and Gift (the life in which the Word goes forth, light in which he is seen, joy in which he is known, generosity wherewith he is bestowed), so in the Son whom the Father generates the depth of the paternal *arche* and the boundless spiritual light and delight of wisdom also inhere, and in the Spirit whom the Father breathes forth the plenitude of paternal being and filial form inhere in the "mode" of accomplished love. Each Person is fully gathered and reflected in the mode of the other: as other, as community and unity at once. Here, in the mystery of divine infinity, one finds, necessarily, a perfect agreement with one another of the languages of "subsistent relations" and of "divine Persons", and a warrant for seeing Trinitarian *vestigia* both in the multiplicit singularity of the soul, which comprises memory, understanding, and will, and so forth, and in the communal implications of each of us in one another, in the threefold structure of love, within which circle we together, as the event of shared love, constitute (however poorly or sinfully) the human "essence". We waver between these two analogical orders at an infinite distance from their supereminent truth; and obviously the orders are not separate: knowledge and love of neighbour fulfil the soul's velleity towards the world, and so grant each of us that internally constituted "self" that exists only through an engagement with a world of others; but that engagement is possible only in that the structure of interiority is already "othered" and "othering", in distinct moments of consciousness' inherence in itself. In the interdependence of these two ways of analogy, enriching and chastening one another, it becomes possible to speak, with immeasurable inadequacy, of the Trinitarian God who is love.

Here, however, we have moved again from the question of the divine image in the soul, through the more ambiguous question of the Trinitarian *vestigia*, back to the question of analogy; but, again, analogical language about God is the effect of a prior divine language, an act of self-disclosure, in which the triune God declares himself "outside" the eternal utterance of himself in his immanent life, in a created likeness. Where I wish, therefore, to direct my gaze in what follows is towards Gregory's understanding of the relationship between the Trinitarian *taxis* and God's image in us, the better to show how, for Gregory, God's own internal life of perfect wisdom, charity, and bliss is (to use the most precise term) *reflected* in the human soul. I hope thus to demonstrate how God's life of light and joy is understood by Gregory as one of radiant "mirroring", to which the being of creation is joined by what might be called, for want of a better term, a "specular economy".

II

Certainly if one were to attempt to isolate the one motif that pervades Gregory's thought most thoroughly, and that might best capture in a single figure the rationality that unifies it throughout, it would be that of the mirror: the surface in which light is gathered, creating depths where none previously existed, and by which it is reflected back to the source of its radiance. One might say, to begin with, that for Gregory all knowledge consists in *theoria* of the reflected, and this is in some sense so even within the life of God: the Son is the eternal image in which the Father contemplates and loves his essence, and thus the Father can never be conceived of without his Son, for were he alone he would have no light, truth, wisdom, life, holiness, or power;[18] "if ever the brightness of the Father's glory did not shine forth, that glory would be dark and blind."[19] This "mirroring" is that one original act of knowledge in which each of the Persons shares; the Only Begotten, says Gregory, who dwells in the Father, sees the Father in himself, while the Spirit searches out the deeps of God.[20] God himself is, one is tempted to say, an eternal play of the invisible and the visible, the hidden Father made luminously manifest in the infinite icon of his beauty, God "speculating" upon himself by way of his absolute self-giving in the other. And it is from this original "circle of glory"[21] that the "logic" of created being unfolds: a specular ontology, according to which creation is constituted as simply another inflection of an infinite light, receiving God's effulgence as that primordial gift that completes itself in summoning its own return into existence. Creation *is* only as the answer of light to light, a created participation in the self-donating movement of the Trinity, existing solely as the manifestation—the reflection—of the splendour of a God whose own being is manifestation: recognition and delight.

Even "material" nature, for Gregory, is entirely subsumed in this economy of reflectivity: the physical world, he says, in its interminable dialectic of constancy and change, stands on the one hand in absolute contrast to divine reality,[22] but, on the other hand, it mirrors within its extraordinary intricacy, magnitude, and inscrutability the incomprehensibility and majesty of God.[23] And the beauty that perdures in the midst of the world's ceaseless becoming excites in the soul a longing for the infinite beauty that it reflects.[24] Indeed, it is not an exaggeration to say that, for Gregory, apart from that reflex of light that lies at creation's heart, there is no world to speak of at all; Gregory, like Basil before him,[25] in various places denies that the world possesses any material substrate apart from the intelligible acts that constitute its perceptible qualities: the world of bodies is a confluence of "thoughts", "bare concepts", "words", noetic "potentialities",[26] proceeding from the divine nature; its *esse*, one might almost say, is *percipi*. The phenomenal realm is not, says Gregory, formed from any underlying matter at all, for "the divine will is the matter and substance of created things (ὕλη καὶ οὐσία τῶν δημιουργημάτων)",[27] the "matter, form (κατασκευή), and power (δύναμις) of the world".[28] The here below, it seems, is like a mirror without tain, a depth that is pure surface, and a surface composed entirely of the light that it reflects. Otherwise said, the physical world is a "primordial, archetypal, and true music", a purely rhythmic and harmonious complication of movements—in which, adds Gregory, human nature can discover an image of itself.[29]

The intelligible creation, however, is an even more thoroughly specular reality. For one thing, all talk of human "nature" most properly refers, in Gregory's thought, not merely to some abstract set of properties instantiated in any given individual, but to the *pleroma* of all persons who come into existence throughout time, who together constitute, as in a single body, the one humanity that God first willed in fashioning a creature in his image,[30] the ideal *anthropos* who dwells eternally in the wisdom and foresight of God, comprehended "altogether in its own plenitude".[31] This alone is truly that "God-like thing (τὸ θεοείκελον χρῆμα)"[32] in whom God has condescended to impress his likeness. When, eschatologically, its temporal unfolding is complete and it is united to the Logos as his pure and glorious body, subjected to the Father, the form of Christ will be proclaimed,[33] made visible in a body stamped with his shape, in whose every part the divine image will shine with equal brightness.[34] Humanity, then, is nothing, either ideally or collectively, apart from its power to display in itself the "form and fashion" of its creator; and this final beauty—this unveiling of the divine likeness—can be glimpsed even now in the church, which Gregory describes as the mirror in which the face of the sun of righteousness, Christ, has become visible within creation, to the wonder and enlightenment even of the heavenly powers.[35] Nowhere, though, does the beauty of the divine image shine forth with a more pristine radiance than in the individual soul purged of sin; for while indeed there will come about, in the eschatological submission of all things to Christ, a coincidence of the beauty of the eternal Logos (who reflects in his depths the full splendour of the unseen Father, in the Spirit's light) and the form of his redeemed creation, still only God can possess that beauty as identical with his essence. Created nature, which is in its inmost essence nothing but change,[36] can manifest God's loveliness only insofar as it continues forever to "capture" it, and continues to preserve within its mutability a dynamism entirely oriented towards God, by which it can grow into an ever greater embrace of divine glory;[37] and this can occur only within the individual will. Rational creation will indeed ultimately come to mirror the splendour of the Logos "in the convergence upon the One Good of all united one to another",[38] and divine beauty will spread throughout all the members of the body, and the grace of the Lord will radiate through all, making everyone of one mind, alike in loveliness, everyone rejoicing in the beauty that appears in one's neighbour;[39] but all of this will come to pass only insofar as each "facet" of that perfect creation will have been purified and made bright within itself with the beauty of holiness.

Hence it is here that the enchantment of the mirror, and its sway over Gregory's theology, reaches its profoundest and most paradoxical intensity: such is the soul's "glassy essence" that it cannot help but assume the aspect of that towards which it is turned, and thus its intrinsic mutability and plasticity make of it also a "stable" surface in which anything—however noble or debased—can be made manifest. Human nature, says Gregory, is a mirror that takes on any appearance, bears the impression of any form, and is moulded solely by the determinations of free will.[40] In its most proper nature, the human mind is in fact that uniquely privileged surface in which the beauty of the divine archetype is reflected and thereby mediated to the entirety of material creation, which is "a mirror of the mirror". Indeed, the lower creation, able to reflect only what humanity reflects, was subjected to the deformity that human nature conceived in itself when it turned towards sin[41] and forsook those endowments—impassibility, beatitude, incorruption —by which the divine image was originally impressed upon it.[42] And we, when humanity languished in the chill of idolatry, assumed in our nature the lifeless coldness of what we worshipped; but, when the sun of righteousness arose, our nature grew warm and lustrous again in his radiance.[43] Now, when our nature draws near to Christ, it becomes beautiful with the reflection of his beauty.[44] Gregory calls the soul a "free and living mirror" that, in gazing upon the face of its lover the Word, is adorned with his comeliness;[45] by looking at him, says Gregory, one becomes what he is.[46] The Word is the bridegroom who tells his bride, the soul, that she has become beautiful by approaching his light and communing with his eternal beauty;[47] and he is also the blinding sun that cannot be looked at directly, but can be glimpsed only in its image: the soul that mirrors his beauty in her own purity.[48] So entirely is the soul's relation to God a matter of this play of light within light, of radiance and reflex, that Gregory can even reverse (or, at any rate, complicate) his specular imagery: just as the bodily eyes cannot see themselves, or perceive their own act of perception, but must find their image outside themselves, in a likeness reflected elsewhere, so the soul that mirrors her divine archetype and his beauty knows herself only in contemplating this reflection, finding in the figure of her archetype the mirror of her own nature.[49]

Obviously, though, in the case of God and the soul, what is reflected immeasurably exceeds the surface in which it appears: the infinite cannot dwell in the finite as a fixed and secure possession (the finite, being nothing but change, cannot even contain itself); God's nature, like a flowing fountain, is inexhaustible and ever new in our sight;[50] but so long as the soul continues to follow after the shining form of the Word, "stretching out" into his infinity, being transformed throughout eternity into an ever more incandescent— ever more divine—vessel of divine glory,[51] she can preserve within her very changeableness a changeless beauty,[52] and display it with an ever fuller splendour. In a sense, the infinity of God's glory is reflected in the insatiable eros it awakens: as the soul always bears the impress of what she mirrors, one glimpse of the divine loveliness leaves an ecstasy ever unexpressed in the depths of the mind, like a longing for the ocean deeps or for the sun, inspired by the lingering taste—mere drops and glimmers—of their beauty.[53] And, no matter how far the soul ventures into the infinity of God, she will continue always to yearn for more of God's beauty, to hunger for his sweetness, nor will she ever find any end to the reality in which she moves[54]—and herein lies the ultimate truth of the soul's similitude to God. Gregory does not distinguish, as other of the fathers do, between God's image and God's likeness in us (between our created "similarity" to the divine and our ultimate assimilation to God in Christ), for such a distinction could have little meaning in his theology. Granted, he often speaks of those proper possessions of rational nature that constitute our aboriginal conformity to the divine, but all of them—including even freedom—exist in us only as reflections of the one good,[55] and only to the degree that we are turned towards it; and this likeness to God is destined to increase in purity, intensity, and resplendency through all eternity. Thus the soul, which is finite but infinitely motile, both is and yet is still called to become the moving mirror of the infinite, in which the glory of God that nothing can comprise and no one see expresses and manifests itself as beauty within change, eternity within movement; and this Gregory calls the θεωρία τῶν ἀθεωρήτων: the contemplation of the inconceivable, the vision of the invisible.[56]

Here, however, we seem not to have advanced beyond paradox, which (despite its often mysterious and even thrilling allure) is, in itself, invariably fruitless and, if left to itself, not a little banal. One could nevertheless bring one's reading of Gregory here to a very plausible close, and be content to see in the "dialectic" between God's infinity and created finitude (between hiddenness and revelation, the invisible and the visible, divine darkness and created light) the entire mystery of the divine image in us; but in doing so one would fail to take account of the deeper truth that allows such a relation—such a proportion between incommensurables—to be a real event both of divine self-disclosure and of creaturely participation in God's goodness. After all, were the relation between God and humanity simply that between the infinitely hidden and the finitely manifest, it would be no relation at all, but only an impossible interval, posed between the ontological and the ontic, the actual and the possible, the absolute and the contingent; its only true proportion would be an infinite otherness, and its only true expression the creature's eternal frustration. There must then already be in God, for Gregory's "dynamist" theology of the image to be meaningful, the ground of possibility that would allow the hiddenness of God at once to remain inviolable and yet to unveil itself in a created icon; there must be a Trinitarian "economy" (to use an entirely inappropriate word, given the infinite self-donation of the Father in the Son and Spirit) of invisibility and disclosure, and the created image of God must participate at once in this invisibility and in this disclosure: it must acquire its brightness "within" the Trinitarian order of relations, according to an economy (the word being here appropriately employed) that, in keeping with Gregory's language, might best be called the economy of glory. And, for Gregory, glory means more than an "attribute" of God: it is his light, his splendour, and—most importantly —his Son and Spirit.

III

There are two distinct, though consequent, senses in which it is correct to speak of the invisibility of God: there is, on the one hand, the sheer infinity of the divine nature, which—flowing from the Father—is the common *proprium* of the divine Persons, who as one forever exceed and excite our souls' most extravagant ecstasies; and there is, on the other hand, that invisibility of the Father within the Trinitarian *taxis* that is altogether convertible with (or, rather, "converted in") the "visibility" or manifestation of the Logos to the Father and the "visibility" or illumination of the Spirit for the Father.[57] The infinity, and so inaccessibility, of God is known to us in both aspects, and it is only because the former invisibility (divine transcendence) proceeds from the latter (the plenitude of the paternal *arche* within the Trinitarian structure of manifestation, of self-outpouring love and self-knowing wisdom) that the restless mutability of our nature can become, by grace, a way of mediation between the infinite and the finite. We can mirror the infinite because the infinite, within itself, is entirely mirroring of itself, the Father's incomprehensible majesty being eternally united to the co-equal "splendour of his glory", his "form" and "impress", in seeing whom one has seen the Father.[58] We can become images of God that shine with his beauty because the Father always has his image in his Son, bright with the light of his Spirit, and so is never without form and loveliness.[59] And (most importantly) the motion of our soul can reflect the eternal peace of God because it can be assimilated to, and made to share in, that one eternal act whereby God is God, by the advent of that act in us under the form of sanctification. Thus, in the surface of the soul, the nature of the Trinitarian life, while always eluding our understanding, somehow appears to us; in his light we see light.

Or, to phrase it differently, God's light is always Trinitarian; his glory is inseparable from his triune being. Moreover, glory, the one indivisible splendour of the Trinity, often figures in Gregory's vocabulary as a special name for the Holy Spirit. This is not to say that divine glory is not a possession of the Father for Gregory, or that Gregory does not, following scripture, call the Son glory, or the splendour of glory, or the seal of glory, who is as inseparable from the Father as is radiance from light.[60] There is, though, a very particular sense in which the light of the Spirit, for Gregory, is that "perfecting" radiance, that fullness of glory, that "completes" the unity of the godhead:[61] when Christ prays, in John 17, according to Gregory, that his followers might be one even as he and his Father are one and indwell one another, and says that the glory that the Father has given him he has given them, he is speaking of the gift of the Holy Spirit; indeed, that glory *is* the Spirit, the glory that the Son had with the Father before the world was made,[62] the "bond of peace" or "bond of unity" (so like the Augustinian *vinculum caritatis*) by which Father and Son dwell in one another, and by which we dwell in God when the Son breathes the Spirit forth upon us.[63] The Spirit, who forever searches the depths of God, and who forever receives from and is sent by the Son, has also always himself possessed his glory, and so has the power to glorify, from everlasting and in infinite superabundance —and "how can any grant the grace of light unless he be himself light?"[64]

Thus the Spirit glorifies the Father and the Son. Nor does he speak falsely who says, "I glorify them that glorify me." "I have glorified you", the Lord says to his Father. And again: "Glorify me with that glory I had with you before the world existed." The divine voice answers: "I have glorified and will glorify." Do you see the revolving circle of glory, from like to like (ἐγκύκλιον τῆς δόξης διὰ τῶν ὁμοίων περιφοράν)? The Son is glorified by the Spirit. The Father is glorified by the Son. Again, the Son has his glory from the Father, and so the Only Begotten becomes the glory of the Spirit. For by what will the Father be glorified if not by the true glory of his Only Begotten? And, again, in what will the Son be glorified if not in the majesty of the Spirit? So, again, our confession and praise, circling back again (ἀνακυκλούμενος ὁ λόγος), glorifies the Son through the Spirit, and through the Son the Father.[65]

This last sentence is of the essence, for it shows that it is this very circle of glory into which the Spirit draws us,[66] and that it is by being refashioned after and in the Trinitarian ordering of self-outpouring light that we are made like God. Thus the "course" of glory in the Godhead—the *taxis* of the divine being—impresses its own reflex in our specular natures, almost under the form of an inversion of the light (as is proper for a mirror), so that God's own loving "return" to himself is our integration into him. Everything —being, power, creation,[67] holiness, love, truth, faith[68]—flows from the Father, through the Son, to the Spirit, and is restored by the Spirit, through the Son, to the Father; and this order of relations, and its doxological dynamism, is the very order of the economy of salvation, which is therefore nothing less than the Trinitarian life gathering us into itself.

In the Song of Songs, says Gregory, when the bride (the soul) cries out that she has been wounded with love, we should see the Father as the archer, sending forth the arrow of his Son, whose "three-pointed arrowhead" has been "dipped in the Spirit of life"; the arrowhead is faith, by which the bolt is fixed deep in the bride's heart; and then (as Gregory astutely observes) the imagery of archery is replaced by that of nuptial delight.[69] That is: as the light of the Spirit appears in the mirror of the soul, the Trinitarian mystery of love becomes manifest; "in this light [human nature] assumes the beautiful form of the dove: that is, the dove that symbolizes the presence of the Holy Spirit."[70] The eyes of the bride are lovely because the dove is reflected in them, and hence they receive the impression of the spiritual life within themselves, so that—thus purified—they are now able to contemplate the beauty of the bridegroom.[71] It is impossible to say Jesus is Lord, or mount in thought to the Son or, through him, to the Father, except in the Holy Spirit.[72]

... there is no means whereby to look upon the Father's *hypostasis* save by gazing at it through its stamp (χαρακτήρ), and the stamp of the Father's *hypostasis* is the Only Begotten, to whom, again, none can approach whose mind has not been illuminated by the Holy Spirit ...[73]

The light of the Father, proceeding in the Holy Spirit, makes the Father's Only Begotten light visible, and so the Spirit's glory makes Father and Son perceptible to our intelligence. Thus, though in one sense it is true that "none has ever seen God", still the grace of the Spirit elevates human nature to the contemplation of God, for "where the Spirit is, there the Son is seen and the Father's glory is grasped".[74] Here, then, in the fused light of holiness—of the Spirit's radiance purifying the soul of every stain and filling her with every splendour—the Trinitarian relations "declare" or "express" themselves, as at once the threefold "community" of glory and also the perfect unity of divine being's structure of infinite self-manifestation: the absolute inseparability of the paternal "depth" from its "image" and "glory".

Moreover, as one considers the sequence of the soul's movements, as the Spirit works upon her, it becomes even clearer that the Trinitarian image appears in us at once as "nature" and as "grace", and appears in each soul as both the ground of "interior" identity and the effect of a transforming act of relation; for the mystery of God's life is reflected not only in the purity of the soul's surface, nor only in the limpid display of the economy of divine revelation there, but also in the "inward" structure of the soul's assimilation to the triune God. Where the light of the Spirit touches the mirror of the soul, one might say, it achieves a chiastic shape; a mirror, after all, not only inverts the light that strikes it, returning it to its source, but also reproduces in itself, under the form of that inversion, the figure of what it faces, thus gathering into itself what it is gathered into. The mirror of the soul is that ideal surface where two depths are reconciled, or where one depth creates another: the infinite light of God, flowing from the Father, through the Son, to the Spirit, and the "spectacle" of its created likeness, rising up from the more "exterior" to the more "interior" aspects of the soul, repeating in the realm of created finitude the infinite's play of hiddenness and manifestation. The three marks of the Christian life, says Gregory, appear in practice, word (λόγος), and thought (ἐνθύμιον); the principle (ἀρχικώτερον) of all three is thought, for mind (διάνοια) is that original source (ἀρχή) that then manifests itself in speech, while practice comes third and puts mind and word into action. It is within this threefold constitution of our essential act of being and manifesting ourselves that we either conceive the image of sin or of Christ, and so we must strive within the circumvolving mutability of our souls to fashion ourselves after the latter; and, when our life is shaped by a mind whose movements are in conformity to Christ, "there is a harmony of the hidden man with the manifest (συμφωνίαν εἶναι τοῦ κρυπτοῦ ἀνθρώπου πρὸς τὸν φαινόμενον)".[75] It is not fanciful, obviously, given the classically "linear" nature of Cappadocian Trinitarianism, to discern a Trinitarian shape in this account of the human soul (of, that is, mind and body); nor is it excessive to speak of a kind of Pneumatological chiasm brought about by the purifying work of sanctification in the soul: inasmuch as the soul's principle, the mind, expresses itself in word and act, moving from full hiddenness to open disclosure, just so the Spirit, meeting us in our fleshly acts and words, conducts the Trinitarian glory "upward" into our thought, refashioning us so that our "depths" are ever more conformed to the brightening "surface" of our natures, making our "return" to ourselves at once a reflex of God's return to himself within his circle of glory and also our ascent out of ourselves—out of our creaturely insubstantiality—into his infinity.

This becomes especially clear in a passage from the *Adversus Macedonianos*: the Spirit, Gregory notes, comes to us first in the life-giving power of baptism, in our flesh, as the power of sanctification; but this requires also a prior act of faith in Christ; but, again, this grace proceeds through the Son from the ungenerate source, the Father, and so faith in the Father somehow comes first. Thus divine life and grace stream down to us from the Father, through the Son, in the perfecting action of the Spirit, and either our praise or our blasphemies return again to the beneficent wellspring of deity, in the Spirit and through the Son; and thus

> ... the pious worshipper of the Spirit sees in him the glory of the Only Begotten and in the Son beholds the image of the infinite [invisible] one,[76] and by this image stamps the archetype upon the mind ... but such is this power that whosoever exalts the Spirit in speech (τῷ λόγῳ) exalts him prior to speech in thought: for speech is not able to ascend alongside thought. When one will have attained to the uttermost extent of human power, to the most exalted thoughts within reach of the human mind, one must still think it inferior to his grandeur ...[77]

Doxology becomes *theoria*, as the words that respond to the Spirit's act within our acts ascends to thought, and thought transcends itself towards God; and, again, the *taxis* of the Trinity shapes the "*taxis*" of the soul, as the ascent of glory from the Spirit and Son back to its paternal source is mirrored in the soul as an ascent from expression to mind. In this way, says Gregory, all duality is overcome, even that between body and soul, so that "the manifest exterior is found in the hidden interior, and the hidden interior in the manifest exterior".[78]

One should note here, however, that this is not simply some barely baptized form of Neoplatonism, according to which the absolute principle emanates itself in diminishing degrees of divinity—from the One, through Nous, to Psyche—and returns to itself in the finite soul's ascent to its own inward and noetic simplicity. Gregory's is not a metaphysics of identity, that would dissolve the divine and human into a bare unity of essence, but a metaphysics of "analogy": of, that is, divine self-sufficiency and its entirely gratuitous reflection in a created likeness. Between God and soul the proportion of the analogy remains infinite. The Father is not a sublime abyss of undifferentiated light; nor is the Son the prism or cymophane in which that light acquires color through its refraction, fragmentation, or distortion; nor is the Spirit that light's delicate and diffuse opalescence here below, waiting to be gathered up again in the soul's contemplative intellect. Gregory's thought is, in a way more radical than any identist idealism could ever be, utterly "speculative". The disproportion between word and thought in us does not reflect any inequality within the simplicity of the divine nature; there is no subordination within God's circle of glory. Moreover, we are drawn into God not by a nisus of the alone to the alone—the reduction of the soul's motion to the austerely featureless light of some "substantial" identity—but by way of ecstasy, of the dynamism of change within a soul that is itself pure change, with no "principle" or "past" to return to or remember. The soul is an absolute futurity,[79] rising up from nothingness into the infinite, forever. We are music moved to music, light born within light, but God dwells in the fullness of his own glory and fellowship, while we reflect that plenitude and love across the infinite distance of imparted glory, in the ever more luminous surface of our mutable nature, both like and unlike the beauty that gives us being and shape, revealing that beauty both in what we are becoming and in the infinity with which it always exceeds the changing mirrors of our souls. Yet, even so, it is here, to this miraculous incommensurability within union between the infinite and the finite, in the dual action (which is really one and the same act) of creation and redemption, that we must look for our images, however insufficient, of God's triune nature.

IV

To return, then, to this essay's beginning: if it is so that this is how the divine image is constituted in us—as the play of God's glory gathering in the mirror of our nature—and that it is a Trinitarian image, then, in considering how God reveals himself in the economy of creation and salvation, we must ultimately find ourselves far beyond all simple oppositions between "social" and "psychological" Trinitarianism, or between "personalism" and "essentialism", or—most certainly—between Greeks and Latins. Just as we must resist every temptation towards those twin reductions of the human essence to either simply society or simply ego (which are vapid as abstractions and vicious as ideologies), we must surely avoid reducing our understanding of God to rudimentary images of either confederacy or subjectivity. In our own souls, in their absolute implication within one another of the exterior and the interior, we discover—without grasping—an icon of that infinite transparency of the divine Persons within and to one another that is also the infinite depth of each divine Person's distinctness. On the one hand, it seems we must understand this infinite coincidence in God of relation and identity by reflecting upon the unity of the soul's motion outward towards expression and inward towards thought (however we may wish to employ "social" models, in themselves they can offer only pictures of extrinsic accommodations between monads, or perhaps of the "transparency" of collective identity, but in neither case can such models account for the mysterious complexity and amphibology of personality, or for the reality of the soul's unity within difference); but, on the other hand, for Gregory no less than for Augustine, the turn inward proves to be, in a still more radical sense, a turn outward: I am an openness whose depth does not belong to me, but to the boundless light that creates me, and whose identity is then given me as other. And as the otherness of God is the soul's true depth, she can possess no identity apart from the otherness of the neighbour; and both the soul's otherness from God and the otherness of each soul from every other reflect the mystery of God's act of "othering" himself within his infinite unity.

It is thus not strange that we find, at the end of Gregory's commentary on the Song, that the bride—who is the figure of the soul joined to Christ the bridegroom—represents also the unity of all souls united to one another in the dove: in the Spirit of glory.[80] The Trinitarian image appears in each soul as she is purified by grace, and then integrally in the body of the Logos, which consists in all of humanity bound with the bond of peace, the very Spirit who is the bond of God's unity. This is an "analogical ontology" in the truest sense: our participation in the being that flows from God is an imparted splendour, always seizing us from nothingness, drawing us into the infinite depth of God's essential simplicity and Trinitarian diversity, into his knowledge and love of his own beauty, but always only insofar as we comprise within our "essence" an interval of incommensurability that is the created likeness of the infinite ontological interval between God and us. That is to say, perhaps still more obscurely, that our likeness to God, posed between the pure ontic ecstasy of our being *ex nihilo* and the infinite ontological plenitude of his being *in se* (between, one might say, our intrinsic nothingness and his supereminent "no-thing-ness"), cannot simply take the form of a homonymy of "attributes" applied to two discrete substances, but must consist, radically, in the rhythm of our difference from him, our likeness to his unlikeness, under the form of a dynamic synthesis of distinct moments of being that, in God, coincide in simple and infinite identity. The distance within us between what we are and that we are, as between our movements *intus* and *foro*, is the necessary expression within the ontic of the distance between God and contingent reality, which distance has as its ontological possibility and *actus* the "distance" that is opened by the eternal act of the hypostatic distinctions within God's unity. I am slipping rather too easily into scholastic terminology. In something more like Gregory's own terms, I should say this: that we are in every way mirrors set among mirrors, within the infinite movement of a light that is always already its own reflection; and in all the complexity of our existence—in moments of interior *theoria* and of exterior communion— we can come to shine with his loveliness, both in the fullness of our nature and in each soul's glorious and ardent thirst for the whole of God's beauty, because in God difference is identity and distinction is unity. Somehow, in this mystery of the moving and finite image of the eternal and infinite God, we are vouchsafed a glimpse of how God knows and loves himself, and is entire in every moment of that act, and receives his glory completely in utterly pouring it forth in another.

Which yields, finally, only this reflection: that a simple, and almost entirely misguided, critical distinction between differing styles of Trinitarianism should have become, over the last century, not only a petrified and petrifying formula in theological scholarship, and not only a justification for pursuing any number of narrower and narrower dogmatic projects, but yet another weapon (and another myth) in the interminable war of recrimination between East and West is an almost excruciating irony. That the language of God's Trinity—of God's perfect unity within the "diversifying" act of his knowing love—should become the grammar of a dispute that seems always to harbour yet greater dimensions of suspicion and misunderstanding is an offense not only against reason, but against love. It may well be that the truest Trinitarian theology of which the Eastern and Western catholic traditions are now capable would consist in the resolution to turn in charity each to the other, in the hope of each finding mirrored in the other those hidden depths that neither is competent to recognize in itself; for the glory of the Spirit is never visible to us apart from our willingness to receive its light from without. Such observations quickly become either saccharine or sanctimonious; so suffice it to remark that no theologian has ever been more adamant than Gregory in insisting that all we are and should be lies outside our grasp, ahead of us, and that we who insist on clinging to our own particular "substances", rather than seeking our proper being in our ecstatic openness to the light that is beyond us, in fact cling to nothing, embrace phantoms, chase shadows and *ignes fatui*, and subjugate ourselves to the transient and empty; and so long as either East or West refuses the glory that appears in the other, it refuses the Holy Spirit—the bond of peace, of unity, and of love—and all our worlds grow dark.

NOTES

1   John Zizioulas, *Being as Communion: Studies in Personhood and the Church* (Crestwood, NY: St. Vladimir's Seminary Press, 1985), p. 40. It has become so lamentably common among my fellow Orthodox to treat the claim of Vladimir Lossky and others that Western theology in general posits some "impersonal" divine ground behind the Trinitarian hypostases, and so fails to see the Father as the "fountainhead of divinity", as a simple fact of theological history (and the secret logic of Latin "filioquism") that it seems almost churlish to note that it is quite demonstrably untrue, from the patristic through the mediaeval periods, with a few insignificant exceptions; honesty, however, not to mention a modicum of shame, moves me to make the observation anyway. It would be comforting to think that only very incautious "scholars"—like the indefatigable polemicist, *provocateur*, and caricaturist John Romanides—fall prey to this error, but one can number even Orthodox theologians of genuine stature and brilliance, like Dumitru Staniloae, among its victims.

2   Théodore de Régnon, *Études de Théologie Positive sur la Sainte Trinité*, 2 vols (Paris 1892), vol. I, 433.

3 Augustine, *De Trinitate* XII.5.5–7.12.
4 Gregory, *Ad Ablabium: Quod non sint tres Dei*, GNO III, I: 40–42.
5 See *De Trinitate* XV.5.7–8. I can do no better than recommend, on this matter, Rowan Williams' quite splendid essay *"Sapientia* and the Trinity: Reflections on the *De Trinitate"* in (eds) B. Bruning, M. Lamberigts, and J. van Houlm, *Collectanea Augustiniana: Mélanges T. J. van Bavel* (Leuven: Leuven University Press, 1990), pp. 317–332.
6 *De Hominis Opificio* XVI, PG 44: 181.
7 Ibid., V, PG 44: 137.
8 Ibid.
9 Ibid., XI, PG 44: 153–156.
10 *De Anima et Resurrectione*, PG 46: 93–96.
11 Since the time of Vladimir Lossky, various modern Orthodox theologians have, in their assault on "filioquism", adopted an exaggerated "Photianism", and argued that between God's acts in the economy of salvation and God's eternal life of generation and procession there is not an exact correspondence of order. See especially Lossky, "The Procession of the Holy Spirit in Orthodox Trinitarian Doctrine", in idem., *In the Image and Likeness of God* (Crestwood, NY: St Vladimir's Seminary Press, 1985), pp. 71–96. This, however, is a theologically disastrous course to tread, and one that leads away from the genuine Orthodox tradition altogether. One might note, to begin with, that were this claim sound, the arguments by which the Cappadocians defended full Trinitarian theology against Arian and Eunomian theology—in works like Basil's *De Spiritu Sancto* and Gregory's *Adversus Macedonianos*—would entirely fall apart; more terribly, however, behind such a severance of the *ordines* of the economic and immanent Trinities from one another lies the quite unexorcisable spectre of nominalism, the reduction of God to some finite being among beings, whose acts could be distinguishable from his nature, whose freedom would be mere arbitrary choice, who would preserve in his being some quantity of unrealized voluntative potential, and whose relation to the being of creation would be one not of self-disclosing revelation, but of mere power—all of which is quite repugnant to patristic tradition. All truth and goodness in creation is a participation in the eternal truth and goodness of God's Trinitarian act of knowledge and love of his own essence, and were any aspect of created reality—especially the economy of salvation—anything but a disclosure of this order of divine reality, it would be neither true nor good (nor, for that matter, real). Surely, if one is seeking a theological argument against the *filioque* clause (as opposed to the perfectly sufficient doctrinal argument that the creed should not have been altered without conciliar warrant), it would be better to point out that it fails adequately to account for other aspects of what is revealed in the economy of salvation: that the Son is begotten in and by the agency of the Spirit as much as the Spirit proceeds through the Son, inasmuch as the incarnation, unction, and even mission (Mark 1:12) of the Son are works of the Spirit, which must enter into our understanding of the Trinitarian *taxis*.
12 Concerning the latter, see Basil, *De Spiritu Sancto*, XLV–VII; concerning the former, *vide infra*.
13 Augustine, *De Trinitate* VI.x.11–12.
14 Gregory, *Ad Ablabium*, 288.
15 *Refutatio Confessionis Eunomii*, GNO II: 403.
16 *Ad Ablabium*, 55–56.
17 As Zizioulas cogently argues: *op.cit*, 89.
18 Gregory, *Contra Eunomium* III.i, GNO II: 32.
19 *Refutatio*, 355.
20 *Contra Eunomium* II, GNO I: 340.
21 See *Adversus Macedonianos: De Spiritu Sancto*, GNO III,I: 109; *Contra Eunomium* I, GNO I: 217–218.
22 *De Hominis Opificio* I, 128–132.
23 *Contra Eunomium* II: 245–254; 260–262.
24 *De Beatitudinibus* IV, GNO VII, II: 121; *De Hominis Opificio* XII, 161–164.
25 Basil, *In Hexaemeron* I,viii, PG 29: 21.
26 See Gregory, *In Hexaemeron*, PG 44: 68–72; *De Anima et Resurrectione*, 124; *De Hominis Opificio* XXIV, 212–213. There are other places, one should note, where Gregory seems to speak of matter more "concretely"—in, for instance, *In Hexaemeron*, 77–80.
27 *In illud: Tunc et Ipse Filius*, GNO II, II: 11.

28 *De Vita Gregorii Thaumaturgi*, GNO X, I: 24.
29 *In Inscriptiones Psalmorum* I.iii, GNO V: 30–33.
30 *De Hominis Opificio* XVI, 185.
31 Ibid., XVII, 189.
32 Ibid., XXII, 204.
33 *Tunc et Ipse Filius*, 20.
34 *De Mortuis oratio*, GNO IX: 63.
35 *In Canticum Canticorum* VIII, GNO VI: 255–257.
36 See *De Anima et Resurrectione*, 141; *In Canticum Canticorum* XII, 351.
37 The idea that the union of the soul—and so of all lower creation—to God consists in a perpetual progress, an *epektasis*, into God's infinity is so utterly characteristic of Gregory's thought that there is little purpose in citing particular passages from his work; I will note, however, that it is the governing theme of the greatest of his spiritual treatises: *In Canticum Canticorum*, *De Vita Moysis* (GNO VII, I), and *De Perfectione* (GNO VIII, I).
38 *In Canticum Canticorum* XV, 466.
39 *De Mortuis*, 66. Cf. Augustine, *De Civitate Dei* XXII, 29–30.
40 *In Canticum Canticorum* IV, 104.
41 *De Hominis Opificio* XII, 161–164.
42 *De Mortuis*, 53.
43 *In Canticum Canticorum* V, 147.
44 Ibid., 150.
45 Ibid., XV, 440.
46 Ibid., II, 68.
47 Ibid., IV, 104.
48 Ibid., III, 90–91; *De Virginitate* XI, GNO VIII, I: 294–297; *De Beatitudinibus* VI, 148.
49 *De Mortuis*, 41; see *In Ecclesiasten* VII, GNO: 411.
50 *In Canticum Canticorum* XI, 321.
51 Ibid., VI, 173–179; VIII, 246, 253; *De Virginitate*, 280–281; *De Perfectione*, 212–214; *Contra Eunomium* I, 112, 285–287; *De Mortuis*, 34–39; *In Inscriptiones Psalmorum* I.v, 39–40; *De Vita Moysis* II, 41–42, 114–118; *et multa cetera*.
52 *De Vita Moysis* I, 32–33.
53 *De Virginitate* X, 289.
54 *De Vita Moysis* I, 4–5; II, 114–118; *De Anima et Resurrectione*, 105.
55 *Oratio Catechetica*, GNO III, IV: 15–20.
56 *In Canticum Canticorum* XI, 326. See ibid., X, 307–311.
57 See *De Perfectione*, 188–189.
58 Ibid., 189.
59 Ibid.
60 *Ad Simplicium: De Fide*, GNO III, I: 63–64.
61 See *Adversus Macedonianos*, 109.
62 *Tunc et Ipse Filius*, 21–22; *In Canticum Canticorum* XV, 466–468.
63 *Tunc et Ipse Filius*, 22; *In Canticum Canticorum* XV, 466–467.
64 *Adversus Macedonianos*, 108.
65 Ibid., 109.
66 See *Contra Eunomium* I, 216–218.
67 *Adversus Macedonianos* 99–100.
68 *Epistula* XXIV, GNO VIII, II: 77.
69 *In Canticum Canticorum* IV, 127–128.
70 Ibid., V, 150–151.
71 Ibid., IV, 105–106.
72 Ibid., 106; *Adversus Macedonianos* 98–99.
73 *Ad Eustathium: De Sancta Trinitate*, GNO III, I: 13.
74 *In Sanctum Stephanum* I, GNO X, I: 90–91.
75 *De Perfectione*, 210–212.
76 The word Gregory uses here is ἀόριστος ("τοῦ ἀορίστου"); as infinity is something Gregory ascribes to all three Persons of the Trinity, as the "measure" of their coequality, it seems somewhat odd to see the Father described as "the infinite"; but Gregory may mean simply that the infinity of the divine essence, flowing from the paternal source, is paradoxically

seen in the Father's coequal image; or it could be that ἀόριστος here carries the force (or may even be a faulty transcription) of ἀόρατος.

77 *Adversus Macedonianos*, 105–107.
78 *De Beatitudinibus* VII, 160–161.
79 *Contra Eunomium* I, 136; *De Anima et Resurrectione*, 93; *In Canticum Canticorum* XII, 366.
80 *In Canticum Canticorum* XV, 466–469.

INDEX

Titles without stated author are by Gregory of Nyssa. Gregory of Nyssa is rendered GN throughout.